Praise for Margaret Renkl's LATE MIGRATIONS

A Read with Jenna/*TODAY Show* Book Club Selection

Winner of the 2020 Phillip D. Reed Environmental Writing Award

Finalist for the 2020 Southern Book Prize

Named a Best Book of the Year by the *New Statesman*, New York Public Library, Chicago Public Library, *Foreword Reviews*, and *Washington Independent Review of Books*

"Beautifully written, masterfully structured, and brimming with insight into the natural world, *Late Migrations* can claim its place alongside *Pilgrim at Tinker Creek* and *A Death in the Family*. It has the makings of an American classic."
—ANN PATCHETT, author of *The Dutch House*

"Magnificent . . . Conjure your favorite place in the natural world: beach, mountain, lake, forest, porch, windowsill rooftop? Precisely *there* is the best place in which to savor this book." —NPR.ORG

"A compact glory, crosscutting between consummate family memoir and keenly observed backyard natural history. Renkl's deft juxtapositions close up the gap between humans and non-humans and revive our lost kinship with other living things."
—RICHARD POWERS, author of *The Overstory*

"Equal parts Annie Dillard and Anne Lamott with a healthy sprinkle of Tennessee dry rub thrown in." —THE NEW YORK TIMES

"[Renkl] guides us through a South lush with bluebirds, pecan orchards, and glasses of whiskey shared at dusk in this collection of prose in poetry-size bits; as it celebrates bounty, it also mourns the profound losses we face every day." —O, THE OPRAH MAGAZINE

"[Renkl] is the most beautiful writer! I love this book. It's about the South, and growing up there, and about her love of nature and animals and her wonderful family." —REESE WITHERSPOON

"*Late Migrations* has echoes of Annie Dillard's *The Writing Life* — with grandparents, sons, dogs and birds sharing the spotlight, it's a witty, warm and unaccountably soothing all-American story."
—PEOPLE

"One of the best books I've read in a long time . . . [and] one of the most beautiful essay collections that I have ever read. It will give you chills." —SILAS HOUSE, author of *Southernmost*

"Reflective and gorgeous . . . I have recommended this book to everybody that I know. It is a beautiful book about love, and [how] . . . to find the beauty in the little things." —JENNA BUSH HAGER, the *TODAY Show*

"This is the story of grief accelerated by beauty and beauty made richer by grief. . . . Like Patti Smith in *Woolgathering*, Renkl aligns natural history with personal history so completely that the one becomes the other. Like Annie Dillard in *Pilgrim at Tinker Creek*, Renkl makes, of a ring of suburbia, an alchemical exotica." —THE RUMPUS

"Like the spirituality of Krista Tippett's *On Being* meets the brevity of Joe Brainard . . . The miniature essays in *Late Migrations* approach with modesty, deliver bittersweet epiphanies, and feel like small doses of religion." —LITERARY HUB

"In her poignant debut . . . Renkl weaves together observations from her current home in Nashville and short vignettes of nature and growing up in the South." —GARDEN & GUN

"*Late Migrations* is a gift, and fortunate readers will steal away to a beloved nook or oasis to commune with its riches. Or they will simply dig into it, unprepared, like the mother with no gardening tools who determinedly pulls weeds until the ground blossoms. They might entrust it to fellow seekers they believe can handle its power. Consecrated, they'll leave initiated into an art of observation lived beautifully in richness, connection, worry, and love." —THE CHRISTIAN CENTURY

"How can any brief description capture this entirely original and deeply satisfying book? . . . I can't help but compile a list of people I want to gift with *Late Migrations*. I want them to emerge from it, as I did, ready to apprehend the world freshly, better able to perceive its connections and absorb its lessons." —CHAPTER 16

GRACELAND, AT LAST

ALSO BY MARGARET RENKL

Late Migrations: A Natural History of Love and Loss

GRACELAND, AT LAST

Notes on Hope and Heartache From the American South

MARGARET RENKL

MILKWEED EDITIONS

Published 2021 by Milkweed Editions
Printed in Canada
Cover design by Mary Austin Speaker
Cover art by Billy Renkl
21 22 23 24 25 5 4 3 2 1
First Edition

Milkweed Editions, an independent nonprofit publisher, gratefully acknowledges
sustaining support from our Board of Directors; the Alan B. Slifka Foundation
and its president, Riva Ariella Ritvo-Slifka; the Amazon Literary Partnership;
the Ballard Spahr Foundation; *Copper Nickel*; the McKnight Foundation;
the National Endowment for the Arts; the National Poetry Series; the Target
Foundation; and other generous contributions from foundations, corporations,
and individuals. Also, this activity is made possible by the voters of Minnesota
through a Minnesota State Arts Board Operating Support grant, thanks to a
legislative appropriation from the arts and cultural heritage fund. For a full listing
of Milkweed Editions supporters, please visit milkweed.org.

Library of Congress Cataloging-in-Publication Data

Names: Renkl, Margaret, author.
Title: Graceland, at last : notes on hope and heartache from the American South
    / Margaret Renkl.
Description: Minneapolis, Minnesota : Milkweed Editions, 2021. | Summary:
    "From New York Times contributing opinion writer and author of Late
    Migrations Margaret Renkl, a selection of her beloved weekly essays pre-
    senting a multifaceted view of the contemporary American South"
    — Provided by publisher.
Identifiers: LCCN 2020054965 (print) | LCCN 2020054966 (ebook) | ISBN
    9781571311849 (hardback) | ISBN 9781571317575 (ebook)
Subjects: LCSH: Southern States. | LCGFT: Essays.
Classification: LCC PS3618.E5766 G73 2021 (print) | LCC PS3618.E5766
    (ebook) | DDC 814/.6--dc23
LC record available at https://lccn.loc.gov/2020054965
LC ebook record available at https://lccn.loc.gov/2020054966

Milkweed Editions is committed to ecological stewardship. We strive to align our
book production practices with this principle, and to reduce the impact of our
operations in the environment. We are a member of the Green Press Initiative, a
nonprofit coalition of publishers, manufacturers, and authors working to protect the
world's endangered forests and conserve natural resources. *Graceland, At Last* was
printed on acid-free 100% postconsumer-waste paper by Friesens Corporation.

For Haywood,
my true home

CONTENTS

Introduction | 1

GRACELAND, AT LAST

INTRODUCTION

These essays—and the op-ed column from which they were drawn—began in grief. I was still mourning my mother's sudden death when my mother-in-law, who had faced Parkinson's disease with grace and courage for eighteen years, finally entered hospice care. Grief and dying governed my days, and there were times when I wondered if I would survive.

Two months before my beloved mother-in-law took her last breath, I ran into Clay Risen, a fellow writer and old friend, at a work event. He asked about my family, and I told him how brutal it is to watch someone you love suffer so terribly. He looked at me for a moment. "Would you ever want to write about that?" he said.

I thought he meant that writing about these terrible times would make them easier, and instantly I wondered why I hadn't opened my notebook and picked up my pen already. For almost my whole life, writing has helped me understand the world, and myself, at least a little bit better. In writing about something unbearable, I somehow find a way to bear it.

Clay is the acclaimed author of six books, but at the time he was also deputy editor of the op-ed section of *The New York Times*. His question, it turns out, wasn't about the psychological benefits of writing. *The Times* was planning a new series about end-of-life issues, and he thought I might want to send an essay to the series editor for possible publication. Against my own misgivings—how could I possibly have time to write something new, in the midst of so much turmoil, that might never see the light of day?—I decided to try.

That essay, published in August 2015, was the first piece I wrote for the paper. It was also the first piece I'd written for any publication in more than five years. Wrestling with that essay for *The Times* made me realize how much I still needed to write, how much I needed to find a way to keep writing. A few months later, I submitted another essay, this one about a backyard territorial dispute between bluebirds and a house wren. *The Times* bought it, too.

And that's how it started: every few months I would send in a new piece of writing—something about the natural world here in Nashville, about growing up in Alabama, or about how it feels to be a red-state liberal—and *The Times* would publish it. In March 2017, the editors offered me a monthly column about "the flora, fauna, politics and culture of the American South." By the end of that year, the column was running every week.

⸺

This opportunity has been a genuine gift, a dream job for any essayist. For a lifelong Southerner writing about the South in a national newspaper, it is also a great responsibility. No other region of the country carries so much cultural baggage, from films like *Gone with the Wind* and *Deliverance* to television shows like *The Beverly Hillbillies* and *Nashville*. Decades of stereotype-driven media have filled this country with people who think they understand Southerners, even if they have never so much as visited this place. But every Monday *The Times* lets me "tell about the South," to borrow from William Faulkner's *Absalom, Absalom!*, and I am inexpressibly grateful for the chance to confront and complicate the stereotypes about my homeland, in as many contexts as I can.

In the years I've been writing for *The Times*, people have often asked me how it feels to be the "voice of the South." That's not a surprising question given the focus of my column. But I'm not the voice of the South, and no one else is, either, because in truth there's no such thing as "the South." The persistent and pervasive notion of this place as a homogenous region, a conservative voting bloc, is as much a product of the American media's imagination as any episode of *The Dukes of Hazzard*.

—

Nevertheless, stereotypes always contain at least a kernel of truth. The legacy of slavery, like the expulsion of Indigenous peoples from their lands, may well haunt Southerners for the rest of time. I understand why people continue to conflate the South today with the states that seceded to maintain their enslavement of other human beings. That original sin, which didn't end in the defeat of the Confederacy but continued through decades of Jim Crow laws, persists today in myriad forms, both overt and subtle.

The South is still a place where white voters in gerrymandered districts consistently elect leaders who are determined to suppress the voting rights of Black citizens, the reproductive rights of women, the housing and employment and family rights of their LGBTQ neighbors, and the citizenship opportunities of the immigrants who do the work—in cities and on farms, in factories and slaughterhouses—that drive Southern economies. Such "leaders" are also working assiduously to privatize public education, destroy unions, undercut climate science, weaken the public health safety net, and execute death row prisoners. All at a breathtaking rate.

But it's worth pointing out that such faults are hardly unique to this region. The political realities of the Southern states hold sway in much of the Midwest, the Plains states, the Southwest, and Alaska, too. And racism, the fault most widely associated with white Southerners, recognizes no regional or international boundary. Just consider how widespread the recent, egregious examples of police brutality against unarmed Black people have been: Louisville but also Minneapolis. North Charleston but also Philadelphia. East Texas but also New York City. Buffalo, Aurora, Cleveland: the list goes on and on.

I don't mean to sound defensive. The fact that the rest of the country shares in the South's greatest moral failing doesn't excuse our brutal history or the way its vestiges linger. But the South has always been more than its most appalling truths. Even during the Civil War—what old-timers still called "the War of Northern Aggression" when I was a child—the South wasn't a monolithic entity. Kentucky, a slave state, officially adopted a position of neutrality during the war. Arkansas joined the Confederacy, but pro-Union residents in Searcy County formed a resistance organization known as "the Arkansas Peace Society." The citizens of Scott County famously seceded from Tennessee rather than from the Union, declaring themselves the "Free and Independent State of Scott." I could keep going, but you get the point.

The South continues to resist easy categorization today. One glance at the final election map of 2020 makes it clear that in many ways the South of the twenty-first century remains deeply rooted in the bloodstained soil of the nineteenth—and yet Virginia and North Carolina have become swing states in national elections, not blocs of solid red. Kentucky elected a Democratic governor. To the vast surprise of everyone but the people actually living there, Georgia flipped to blue in the presidential race.

Perhaps most crucially, an election map can't tell you what people are actually like. It doesn't even tell you what the people who consistently vote for charlatans and scoundrels are actually like. Human beings are always more complex than the way they vote could ever suggest. People can be good and bad, brilliant and hopelessly short-sighted, empathetic and willfully blind. This is both the glory and the tragedy of human nature: we are not simple creatures. If Americans understood that basic fact, they would not have been so surprised to learn that more Latinx and Black people voted for Donald Trump in 2020 than in 2016.

The problem with trying to typecast an entire region is not just that red states aren't confined to the American South, or that the American South itself isn't reliably red, or that Southern voters are motivated by varied and complex priorities. It's that there is no one South in the South. The Deep South is as different from the Mid-South and the Upper South as the Mid-South and the Upper South are from each other. The urban South looks far more like its counterparts in the urban North and the urban West than it does the rural counties in its own states. The coastal South and the mountain South might as well be two separate countries. The immigrant South overlaps them all, multifarious in too many ways to list.

I can't accurately represent every one of these Souths, and I wouldn't dare try. As an essayist, all I can do is write from my own experience about how complex our homeland is. All I can

5

do is try to make it clear that there is far more to this intricate region than many people understand.

—

This book will introduce a variety of Southerners: Black and white and brown, urban and rural, religious and anti-religious, conservative and progressive, infuriating and inspiring. Their stories are perhaps more uplifting than enraging because I want this book to give a sense of how many people here are working for positive change.

You will meet an urban shepherd who clears sensitive landscapes of invasive vegetation; a group of teenagers who organized a youth march for Black Lives Matter; a journalist who carries on the work of Martin Luther King Jr. in the city where Dr. King was murdered; and a Tennessee Department of Transportation employee whose vision turned the entire state's roadsides into pollinator gardens. You'll meet neighbors standing in support of immigrants; nonprofits working to protect the environment; church parishioners sheltering the homeless; and poets and novelists and dancers and song-writers whose work teaches us to see the complicated truth of a place that can be confounding.

Many, many people are trying to make things better here—people who recognize evil when they see it and are working to vanquish it; people who understand that hate is sometimes a carapace for pain and who haven't given up hope of turning hatred into love. In my column I try to dedicate as many words to celebrating the heroes as I do to calling out those who are making trouble for so many others. People in the South are both damaged and damaging, but they are not only those things.

—

In putting together this collection, I considered a number of different organizational plans. One was a narrative account of the roughly four years the book covers. Another grouped essays by approach: personal, reported, and a hybrid of both. A third divided the essays into time frames: remembrances of the past, reports of life today, and speculations about what the future might hold as climate change reshapes the earth.

But I decided instead to think of this book as a kind of patchwork quilt, the art form of my maternal ancestors. Quilting is still an art, but today's quilts tend to be constructed from materials purchased expressly for that purpose, carefully matched and color-coordinated, while the patchwork quilts of old came from scraps of repurposed fabric: clothes so worn out they could not be repaired again, flour sacks and livestock feed bags, ragged sheets and blankets, the tiniest bits of material left over from making a new dress. For the Alabama women who raised me, a quilt was a time capsule that brought the past into both the present and the future. Many of the quilts they made now lie in a cedar chest at the foot of my bed here in Tennessee, nearly a hundred years after their creation.

This collection is a patchwork that is both time-inconsistent and made of mismatched parts because it's impossible to present a single, comprehensive portrait of the American South. It's also impossible to present a single, comprehensive portrait of one writer's experience—especially when that experience is conveyed in unrelated essays over the course of years.

You'll see dates on these pieces because the world changed rapidly and profoundly during the time when I was writing them. Some of what I predicted, like the wholesale betrayal Trump voters would feel when they realized they'd been duped, never materialized—the former president's base remained firmly behind him even as a mismanaged pandemic wrecked their livelihoods and killed their fellow Americans by the hundreds of thousands. Some of the fears I wrote about have turned out to be far worse than my own dark imaginings, particularly as the long-predicted climate emergency has become a climate cataclysm.

In the end, I arranged the essays by the categories to which I frequently return. There are sections on the flora, fauna, politics, and culture of the American South, of course, but also on the imperiled environmental context in which the flora and fauna are trying to survive, the social justice issues raised by the politics of this region, and the rich artistic life of a widely varied culture.

—

Running throughout the book, as well, are more personal matters—stories from my own family, questions of faith and community—because kinship and religion have always been fundamental to life in the South. In my childhood, families often belonged to the same congregation for generations, so church was the acknowledged center of social life. That may be less true for Southerners today, as rural livelihoods disappear and more people settle far from the places where they grew up, but it's still impossible to write about the Bible Belt without at least acknowledging the pervasive reach of Christianity.

I often find myself explaining to people outside the South that the fundamentalists and evangelicals who dominate the conversation aren't the only Christians living here, and that

Christians aren't the only believers here, either. Christian conservatives are widely known for legislating sexuality and gender issues, but religious people who focus on the social justice message of the Gospels live here, too. They join Black Lives Matter protests; they pray outside prisons on execution days; they defend the rights of their LGBTQ neighbors; they work to protect the environment; they welcome immigrants. They are rarely in the news, so some of these columns describe the work their faith—my own faith—calls us to do.

Other essays touch on my family's history, both because it's only fair that readers should have some way of knowing how I came to stand where I stand, and because my own life straddles one of this country's great divides: the one that exists between people who live in tiny towns, or no town, and people who live in diverse cities. Every state in the red South has at least one blue city or college town. Think of Atlanta; think of New Orleans; think of Austin; think of Oxford, Mississippi, and the research triangle of North Carolina. Think of Nashville. These are the proverbial blue dots in a red sea.

Many of these columns highlight what's happening in Nashville, and that's for obvious reasons: I live here, and this is the community I know most intimately. But I never write about Nashville for the sake of writing about Nashville. I write about what's happening here only when it echoes what is happening across the region, or the country. When the Tennessee General Assembly limits the ability of Nashville leaders to pass progressive laws, you can be sure the same thing is happening in Texas and Georgia and North Carolina, too.

And while I live in twenty-first-century Nashville, a growing and diverse urban center, I come from deeply rural Alabama. That land and those people formed me, and I still feel as much a part of their world as of the city where I have lived for nearly thirty-five years. Visiting the farming community where my parents are buried, or the small town where my husband's family is from, I feel the same way every time I leave a four-lane highway for a country road: the crunch of tires turning onto a battered back-road blacktop is the sound of coming home.

—

Finally, the South is more than the people who live here. It is also the unfathomable natural beauty of a place that is still predominately rural and very often wild. This is a gorgeous land shot through with rivers running like lifeblood through ancient mountains and old-growth forests, through limestone bluffs and grassy balds, through black-belt farms and red-dirt wiregrass and salty coastal plains and marshy places fluttering with life. Even now, as the ravages of climate change become more and more evident, much of this land is more beautiful than you could possibly believe unless you've seen it with your own eyes.

The South has always been so bound up in both beauty and suffering that it isn't possible to untangle one from the other. I think that's why this region keeps giving birth to more than its fair share of writers. To love a person is always to love in spite of the faults that intimacy reveals, and so it is with a place. To love the South is to see with clear eyes both its terrible darkness and its dazzling light, and to spend a lifetime trying to make sense of both.

FLORA
& FAUNA

HAWK. LIZARD. MOLE.
HUMAN.

Because William Blake was right:
"Every thing that lives is holy."

August 31, 2020

HAWK.

One of my sons noticed it before the rest of us did: a hawk perched on the edge of the birdbath mounted to our deck rail, only a few feet from the back door. One yellow claw gripped the edge of the shallow bowl; the other claw was curled up and tucked into the bird's breast feathers as though for sleep. It was the middle of a bright Sunday afternoon, but the hawk had settled in for a stay. Its coloring—the brown streaking, the pale eyes—indicated a young Cooper's hawk, not long out of the nest.

Food is abundant during these hot, dry days, but water is not, and many thirsty creatures make use of this birdbath. As we were marveling over the hawk, a young squirrel came around the edge of the nearest maple tree and leapt lightly onto the railing, heading over for a drink. It saw the hawk and stopped for a moment to look it over. Then, unbelievably, the squirrel continued to make its way toward the birdbath. The three humans standing at the back door all gasped.

Cooper's hawks belong to the genus *Accipiter*, avian predators capable of immense speed and built to navigate

13

dense vegetation in pursuit of prey. My field guide, Pete Dunne's *Birds of Prey*, calls the Cooper's hawk "a slate-backed, torpedo-shaped cruise missile of a raptor." These birds eat mostly other birds, and they can be the bane of backyard bird-watchers because they often stake out feeders. It is terrible to watch what happens when a Cooper's hawk kills a songbird—the explosion of feathers, the piteous cry.

At first the hawk remained in its resting position, but I wish you could have seen what happened to its eyes when it saw that squirrel. Its head turned; I swear I could see its pupils dilate.

The baby squirrel was lucky that this was a baby hawk: a goofy, inexpert chase scene unfolded in the maple tree, with no harm come to the squirrel, but already there was a focused savagery in that young bird's eyes that I have never seen before except in photos and film. A thrilling ferocity—dangerous and urgent. Utterly, beautifully, inescapably wild.

LIZARD.

On the other side of the house, a skink has taken up residence under the low ramp my husband built for his elderly father's scooter chair. The ramp is covered with old roofing shingles, and last spring, when the skink was carrying eggs, she took to lying on those sun-warmed shingles and sprawling out like a teenager on a pool raft, or Superman in flight: arms extended, legs stretched out behind her. The broadhead skink is the largest lizard native to the Southeast, reaching up to thirteen inches in length. The skink who shares our front stoop is well past half that size.

Broadhead skinks are attentive mothers, and ours disappeared for a few weeks in early summer, presumably to lay her eggs and guard them till they'd safely hatched. I was afraid a feral cat had caught her, but she's back now, and from time to time a miniature striped skink with a blue tail will join her on the stoop. It may be one of her babies, though of course I can't be sure.

Broadhead skinks are often found in trees, but this one rarely leaves the shelter of our ramp except to hunt or to sun, and the spot she has picked out is rich in insects, so she needn't range far. When she's startled, she darts more quickly than you could possibly believe, but when she prowls, she moves in an undulation that mimics the gliding of a snake. I have watched delivery drivers jump back at the sight of her.

I like to watch our resident skink while she's sunning, the way she looks up at me through the glass of the storm door, fully aware that I'm watching her. If I open the door, she'll scoot under the ramp on reptilian principle, but she has learned that I am not a threat. Once she's safely under cover, she'll poke her head back out to see what I'm up to. There is such transparent intelligence in her eyes.

Really, it's just one eye, for she always tilts her head sideways to look at me, exactly the way a songbird would. When I walk out front to feed the bluebirds, I always toss a few worms into the ground cover for the furtive house wrens, who, though ferocious, can't compete with an entire bluebird family. The wrens are quick, but the skink, waiting at the stoop at the exact right time of day, always helps herself to a worm or two before the wrens even realize I've come outside.

MOLE.

I haven't actually seen a mole, but a mole lives here. Beyond the front stoop, its tunnels crisscross our yard, and walking there becomes an exercise in sinking. We once had a terrier mix named Betty who spent all autumn digging up mole runs. Every year she managed to make our yard look like someone had been conducting trench warfare there.

Millie, our current terrier mix, has never shown the first inclination to dig anywhere or to hunt anything, so the current mole remains unmolested. There are spots all over our yard where the mole has opened up a hole in the earth to push out the loose soil it has excavated in making its tunnels, or where its offspring have exited the tunnel in search of their own territories: as I learned from Marc Hamer's wonderful memoir *How to Catch a Mole: Wisdom from a Life Lived in Nature*, hands down the most charming book I read in 2019, moles are combative, solitary creatures except during mating, and their youngsters don't hang around.

Moles can wreck the appearance of a poisoned, sprinkler-watered lawn, but they have never done any harm to this scruffy, wildlife-friendly patch of ground. Many wildflower seeds require disturbed soil to germinate and take root, and molehills are a safe landing place for wildflower seeds carried on the wind. Meanwhile the mole is busy underground doing its useful work: aerating the soil and consuming vast quantities of worms, slugs, and grubs—often eating its own body weight in a day. A resident mole is always better pest control than any exterminator, and I will always choose a living creature over any field of poisoned grass.

HUMAN.

How lucky I am to live in a home with windows. Against all odds—the encroachments of construction companies and lawn services and exterminators—these windows still open onto a world that stubbornly insists on remaining wild. I love the bluebirds, and I also love the murderous hawk who reminds me that the peace of the backyard is only a fiction. I love the lizard who looks so much like a snake, and I also love the snake who would eat her if it could.

And my friend the mole, oh how I love my old friend the mole. In these days that grow ever darker as fears gather and autumn comes on, I remember again and again how much we all share with this soft, solitary creature trundling through invisible tunnels in the dark, hungry and blind but working so hard to move forward all the same.

THE FLOWER THAT CAME
BACK FROM THE DEAD

The Tennessee coneflower is proof that much of nature might yet recover—if we commit ourselves to change.

Ｊ𝖴ＮＥ 24, 2019

Certain old-fashioned words from fairy tales and storybooks still cling to me from childhood. *Moor. Vale. Bog. Glade.* For a child, such words conjure magical places—untouched, holy lands where fairies might live and animals might speak in ways I understand. Not long after I moved to Tennessee, I heard the term "limestone cedar glade" for the first time and immediately thought again of magic. But I've been here almost thirty-two years now, and until last week I had never visited the site of one of conservation's greatest success stories: the Tennessee coneflower.

This unassuming purple flower belongs to the genus *Echinacea*. It grows in a miniature ecological niche—the limestone barrens and cedar glades of Tennessee's Davidson, Rutherford, and Wilson Counties. In limestone cedar glades, rock formations lie so close to the surface that the soil is too shallow for the kinds of trees that grow in the deciduous forests surrounding the glades. Instead, this stony land supports vegetation more typical of grasslands or deserts, including uncommon wildflowers: limestone fameflower, limestone glade milkvetch, cedar gladecress, glade savory, glade violet, glade bluet, and a host of others.

The star of the cedar glades of Middle Tennessee is the Tennessee coneflower. First identified as a distinct species in 1898, it was for decades assumed to be extinct. In 1968 it was rediscovered by Elsie Quarterman, a legendary Vanderbilt botanist, who immediately went to work to protect it. The Tennessee coneflower became one of the first plant species added to the endangered species list.

Through the combined efforts of Dr. Quarterman, the Tennessee chapter of the Nature Conservancy, the Tennessee Department of Environment and Conservation, the National Park Service, and the US Fish and Wildlife Service, as well as many private and corporate donors, the Tennessee coneflower population rebounded. It was removed from the endangered species list in 2011. Dr. Quarterman attended the delisting ceremony at Cedars of Lebanon State Park. She was a hundred years old.

The Tennessee coneflower is not the only species to return from the dead. Other so-called Lazarus species include the New Guinea highland wild dog, the Nelson's small-eared shrew, the Azuay stubfoot toad, the takahe bird, and the Bocourt's terrific skink, just for starters. (There is also some hope for the Formosan clouded leopard, with a number of yet-to-be-confirmed sightings reported recently in Taiwan.) Each one reminds us that recovery is sometimes possible, even for a species believed to be lost forever.

When I made up my mind to visit one of Tennessee's lime-stone cedar glades to see the Tennessee coneflower for myself, I wasn't sure where to start. Today there are thirty-five colonies of the plant spread out across six different populations in Middle Tennessee, and some are far more accessible than others. So I called the Tennessee Division of Natural Areas and reached David Lincicome, manager of Tennessee's Natural Heritage

Inventory Program, which tracks rare and endangered species in the state. He recommended a trip to the Couchville Cedar Glade, which has one of the largest populations of the Tennessee coneflower. This particular colony is also easily reached via a level footpath, no GPS device required.

I knew what a limestone cedar glade is supposed to look like—more like a desert than the magical forest clearings of European fairy tales. But I was caught off guard by the alien nature of the landscape I found. The limestone glade is ringed by a kind of prairie—grasslands blooming outrageously with wildflowers: gray-headed coneflowers and Queen Anne's lace and butterfly weed and pasture roses.

There were thousands of Tennessee coneflowers blooming all over the grasslands, too, and like the other wildflowers they were covered with bumblebees and butter-flies. But what amazed me was the way they also bloomed right in the rocky barren of the limestone glade itself. They grew in the middle of the rocky path next to the prickly pear, Tennessee's native cactus. They popped up out of what seemed to be solid stone. I would not have been more surprised to find flowers blooming on the moon.

There's a great danger in hope, as Roxane Gay has pointed out: "Hope allows us to leave what is possible in the hands of others," she writes in *The New York Times*. "When we hope, we have no control over what may come to pass. We put all our trust and energy into the whims of fate. We abdicate responsibility. We allow ourselves to be complacent."

It's no doubt a mistake to believe that everything will work out in the end. At the moment, everything is far, far from working out. But there's as great a danger in despair as there is in unwarranted hope. Despair tells us that there's no point in fighting, that there's nothing to be done but surrender and make peace with the consequences. And if the consequences mean losing 50 percent of the world's surviving species, well, what's to be done?

The lowly Tennessee coneflower tells us there *is* something to be done. It will not be easy, and it will cost money. It will not be solved by government alone, by the market alone, by advocacy alone, or by personal responsibility alone. It will require everything we have, all the resources we can marshal.

But it can be done. The Tennessee coneflower reminds us that it can still be done. A flower that for decades was believed to be gone forever now grows in great profusion on what appears to be pure rock. If ever there was a Lazarus flower, this would surely be it—brought back from the dead, thriving in stone.

THE EAGLES OF
REELFOOT LAKE

*Maybe the reason we love these birds so much
is that we almost lost them.*

I n the far northwest corner of Tennessee, just this side of the
Mississippi River, lies a landscape like no other. Reelfoot
Lake is less a lake than a system of bayous, creeks, and
swampland connected by areas of shallow open water. It was
created in the winter of 1811–1812, when a series of powerful earthquakes and aftershocks caused fifteen thousand acres
of cypress forest to sink. The waters of the Mississippi River
rushed into the depression. To eyewitnesses, the river seemed
to be flowing backward.

Reelfoot's average depth is barely more than five feet,
and the stumps of hundreds of thousands of drowned trees
lie just beneath its surface. Even today, more than two hundred years later, it can be unclear where the lake begins and
ends. Even the names of its geographical features suggest a
porous relationship between land and water: Big Ronaldson
Slough. Horse Island Ditch. Buck Basin. Keystone Pocket.

Hundreds of bald eagles surround the lake, perched in
bald cypress trees. (That both are "bald" is a coincidence.)
Their yellow feet grip the black branches; their yellow eyes
are trained on the lake. They are watching for the slippery
shadows of fish moving beneath the dark water. They are
watching for the splash of a duck landing on the lake.

I came to Reelfoot Lake State Park because it—along with the Reelfoot National Wildlife Refuge, which covers the northern part of the lake—is the "eagle-watching headquarters for the whole country," according to Warren Douglas, a park ranger. The lake is a crucial wintering ground for migratory waterfowl, and that makes it prime hunting territory for eagles.

"The colder it is, the more ducks and geese migrate south, and eagles usually follow the snow geese because snow geese are the easiest food to catch," Mr. Douglas explained. "The colder the winter, the more eagles we have here."

But the climate is growing warmer now, and this year the waterfowl stayed away until late in the season. "It's been so warm this winter we didn't have one duck on this refuge till the day after duck season ended," Mr. Douglas said. "Finally an arctic front came through, and within days we went from a thousand ducks here to a million."

In addition to the migratory eagles, several hundred eagles live at Reelfoot year-round, including about a hundred nesting pairs. Bald eagles typically mate for life, and each pair frequently uses the same nest again and again, adding a new layer of branches and sticks each year. A bald eagle's nest can weigh more than two tons. From a distance, it looks as though someone has hauled a Ford Explorer into the sky and lodged it in the fork of a tree.

It would be hard for me to explain why I so badly wanted to see an eagle on the nest, badly enough that my husband and I had been planning this trip since last summer. I am not particularly inclined to anthropomorphize nature, and to me an eagle on the wing is no more majestic than other large, soaring birds. They are not more beautiful than pelicans flying in formation, or great blue herons gliding over a lake, or vultures riding an air current high in the sky. And I am fully aware that watching a bald eagle pull a fish from the water is not fundamentally different from watching a bluebird pluck a beetle from the grass.

And yet there *is* something different about this bird, something that made the Second Continental Congress adopt it as the new nation's emblem—over the objection of Benjamin Franklin. "He is a Bird of bad moral Character," Franklin wrote in a letter to his daughter. "He does not get his Living honestly. You may have seen him perched on some dead Tree near the River, where, too lazy to fish for himself, he watches the Labour of the Fishing Hawk; and when that diligent Bird has at length taken a Fish, and is bearing it to his Nest for the Support of his Mate and young Ones, the Bald Eagle pursues him and takes it from him."

Mr. Franklin was not wrong about the bald eagle's opportunistic nature, but the rest of us still love them. During nesting season, all across the web, hundreds of thousands of people are watching wildlife cameras trained on eagles' nests. Since 2007, a pair of bald eagles in Decorah, Iowa, has reliably produced three eggs a year and raised their eaglets under the watchful eyes of anyone with internet access—more than 370 million viewers so far. When tragedy struck last year— the male disappeared without a trace, leaving the female to raise their chicks alone—the Raptor Resource Project, which maintains the camera, held a Facebook memorial service for the beloved bird. (The female has taken a new mate this year and is laying eggs again.)

For years it looked as though we would be forced to hold a memorial service for the species itself.

Eagles exist at the top of the food chain. If a fish or a duck has poison in its system and the bald eagle eats it, the eagle is eating the poison, too. In the mid-twentieth century, run-off carrying the insecticide DDT entered so many rivers and streams that eagles were regularly eating contaminated fish, which caused them to lay eggs with shells too thin to support incubation. In addition, eagles often died of poisoning when they ate waterfowl injured by lead shot. And habitat loss compromised the nesting opportunities of even healthy birds.

When the bald eagle was adopted as our national emblem, an estimated 100,000 pairs were nesting in what later became the lower forty-eight states. By 1963, only 417 nesting pairs remained.

Thanks in large part to Rachel Carson's book *Silent Spring*, concerted efforts were finally made to protect the remaining bald eagle population. DDT was banned for most uses in 1972, and lead shot was phased out for waterfowl hunters in 1991. Those measures were ultimately successful, and the bald eagle was removed from the endangered species list in 2007. It remains protected under a number of federal statutes, including the Bald and Golden Eagle Protection Act and the Migratory Bird Treaty Act, which make it illegal to kill or disturb eagles or their nests.

In one way of looking at it, the bald eagles at Reelfoot Lake are returning the favor by providing a critical source of income for the region. Once a thriving community of farmers—upward of twenty-five thousand at midcentury, Mr. Douglas said—the area is now home to a few thousand residents (not including the inmates at the Northwest Correctional Complex). The fertile land in the Mississippi floodplain is still farmed, but mechanization has replaced human labor. Across Lake County there are ghost churches at crossroads and the corners of fields; once the center of community life, they've fallen into ruin, and the county has become one of the poorest in the United States.

Tourism is now its main source of income. Sportsmen keep the rental rooms filled during hunting and fishing seasons. Birders and naturalists arrive during the songbird migrations. And in winter, eagle watchers show up from around the world to see a gorgeous bird, its talons extended, snatch a duck from a fallow rice field or sit quietly on a nest at the top of an immense cottonwood tree, its gleaming feathers rustling in the wind.

On our last morning at Reelfoot, our fellow guests at the Dragonfly Inn were speculating at breakfast about why so many people are fascinated by eagles. "I think it's because they're so big," one woman said. "So majestic." Another woman looked at a preacher who happened to be sitting at the head of the table. "It's Isaiah, isn't it?" she asked. "'But those who wait for the Lord shall renew their strength, they shall mount up with wings like eagles, they shall run and not be weary, they shall walk and not faint.'" He nodded.

Maybe it's both. To see an eagle on the wing is to see something magnificent, to be reminded of the nature of eternity. But here on earth, these glorious creatures are wholly mortal—as fragile and as temporary as every one of us—and I liked my husband's theory best of all. "It's because we almost lost them," he said. "It's because we almost lost them, but we learned our lesson just in time. Before it was too late."

THE REAL ALIENS IN OUR
BACKYARD

*The future of this country's wild spaces may depend
on changing the way suburban Americans
think about plants.*

MARCH 11, 2019

O ur yard is separated from our backdoor neighbors'
yard by a small city easement. For the first two
decades we lived in this house, our elderly neighbors kept a deep border of hardwood trees and woody
shrubs on their side of the easement, a shelter for songbirds
and a corridor for wildlife—deer and opossums and rat
snakes and box turtles and red foxes and great horned owls,
among many others.

When those neighbors died, developers bought their house
and tore it down. Then they cleared the lot, edge to edge. The
mature trees and plants in the easement weren't bulldozed, but
many of them died anyway, killed by the weight of construction
equipment lumbering across their roots.

But nature, as you may have heard, abhors a vacuum,
and new plants have sprung up in the easement: privet and
bush honeysuckle and wintercreeper and a host of other
shrubs and vines. With so many of the big trees gone now,
more sunlight reaches the new plants, and they have grown
like something possessed, something determined to fill the
gaps left by all the red maples, hackberries, poplars, and
cedars lost to development in this neighborhood.

You'd think I'd be happy about all this green life. You'd think I'd be grateful that the warblers have a new place to rest on their long migration. But I'm not happy. I'm discouraged.

This kind of nature isn't natural. Most of the plants now growing at the back of our lot aren't native to Middle Tennessee. They're native to other continents entirely. As aliens, they are poor food sources for our native animals and insects. A landscape populated by nonnative plants is, for wildlife, the equivalent of a desert. Worse, many alien plants are also highly invasive, choking out native plants and sending out their own seeds, some of which will settle and grow in wild places miles away from suburbia.

During summer, the easement behind my house *looks* as healthy and verdant as any natural place left to its own devices, but it's nothing of the kind. The invasive plants are far too big for me to dig up, but I do my best to minimize the damage—cutting back buds before they can flower, pulling up seedlings, planting native trees and shrubs where I can. The project often feels Sisyphean.

That's why I ended up tagging along with Frances Corzine on a cold, drizzly Saturday morning this month as she checked on the progress of Weed Wrangle, a coordinated effort to eradicate invasive plants in public parks and natural areas. The initiative was founded in 2015 by the Garden Club of Nashville with funding from the Garden Club of America's Partners for Plants program. With the national club's sponsorship—and the help of community partners like the Tennessee Environmental Council and Tennessee's state park system—it has grown like kudzu, spreading to sixty other cities in Tennessee and to twelve other states.

This does not reflect well on me, but I have always associated the term "garden club" with tea roses and insecticides, pristine lawns and herbicides. When I confessed to being surprised by the garden club's interest in conservation, Ms. Corzine laughed. "We're not your grandmother's garden club," she said.

Clearly not. At Fort Negley, the site of a Civil War–era Union fort and the first Weed Wrangle site on Ms. Corzine's list that morning, volunteers were spread out along stone fortifications on the hillside, gently removing ailanthus seedlings. At fragile historic sites, invasive plants like ailanthus, inappropriately nicknamed "tree of heaven," pose a risk not only to wildlife and native plants but also to the site itself, as roots push apart the stones of the buildings that preservationists are working so hard to save.

Over at Nashville's City Cemetery, our second stop, volunteers wielding a contraption I'd never seen before were attacking a bank of bush honeysuckle. An Uprooter, it turns out, is a miracle tool, part wrench and part lever, that makes it possible for a normal person to pull a sapling out of the ground by its roots. It dawned on me that if every homeowner in the country kept an Uprooter in the toolshed next to the lawn mower, the spread of invasive plants could be greatly slowed.

The relationship between backyard plants and the health of the nation's wild spaces is a point that Cayce McAlister, president of the Garden Club of Nashville, was careful to make when I spoke with her by phone last week. Ms. McAlister was the inciting force behind Nashville's first Weed Wrangle and is now an organizer of the national club's efforts to help the program grow, eradicating invasive plants and replacing them with native varieties nationwide.

The idea for Weed Wrangle came to her when she took some garden-club guests from Oregon on a tour of Warner

Parks, the three-thousand-acre crown jewel of Nashville's extensive system of parks and greenways. Ms. McAlister was lamenting all the bush honeysuckle, Bradford pear trees, Chinese privet, and English ivy growing in that beautiful wildness, when her guests pointed out the same plants growing in nearby neighborhoods. That's when Ms. McAlister had her brainstorm: "If we don't tell people what these plants are, we'll never get them out of our parks."

But Americans are still buying nonnative plants, even highly invasive ones, from local nurseries and big-box garden centers alike. "Privet grows. Honeysuckle grows," Ms. McAlister points out. "And people come back for more because it grows."

Unless they learn not to. During the first four years of Weed Wrangle's existence—in a total of four mornings' work—volunteers removed more than 150,300 invasive plants across Tennessee. But the benefits of the program expand far beyond the communal effort itself. "Volunteers have fun doing it, but the most important thing is that they go home and do the same thing in their own yards," Ms. Corzine said. "And then they tell their neighbors."

MAKE AMERICA
GRAZE AGAIN

Nashville's Zach Richardson uses sustainable practices—
and a flock of sheep—to clear overgrown landscapes.

APRIL 22, 2019

J ust past the intersection of Highway 70 and Old Hickory
Boulevard, in the Bellevue section of Nashville, stands a
pocket of native wilderness. Four acres of pristine wood-
land tucked behind a condominium complex, the Belle Forest
Cave Arboretum is a stone's throw from restaurants, shops,
and big-box stores. I've passed it probably a hundred times
over the years with no idea it was there.

Last week, on a drizzly spring afternoon, I found it. The
pocket park provides the perfect habitat for a huge range of
plant and animal life: in addition to the usual songbirds,
mammals, turtles, and wildflowers that can make a home of
even the tiniest wooded opportunity, Belle Forest boasts sal-
amanders and tricolored bats and at least thirty-nine species
of trees.

It is also home to a wide range of invasive plants: bush
honeysuckle and Chinese privet and many others that pose a
serious threat to native plants and the wildlife that depends
on them. But clearing this densely woven environment of
unwanted vegetation, especially without harming native
plants, is a challenge: herbicides would poison the creeks,
and heavy machinery would dislodge the trees and compact
the soil—if machinery could even make it up the steep terrain.

That's where Zach Richardson comes in. Mr. Richardson, thirty years old, is a Nashville native who holds a master's degree in landscape architecture from the University of Georgia. He also owns a flock of sheep that he deploys all over the city to manage invasive vegetation in a safe, ecologically sensitive, and cost-effective way. The Nashville Chew Crew, as he calls his flock, will eat even the most noxious invasive plants: kudzu, mimosa, English ivy, euonymus, Bradford pear, you name it.

Mr. Richardson is a passionate and articulate advocate for this ancient method of land management, not just in fragile areas like the Belle Forest Cave Arboretum, but also in public parks and greenways, vacant city lots and suburban backyards. His sheep, he says, "are easy on the land," leaving the topography undisturbed and the soil enriched. ("They fertilize as they go," he points out.)

They're also adorable. A day-old lamb leaping behind its mama in the mild light of springtime is about as close to beatific as anything you will see in this life.

That cuteness factor, while providing no direct environmental benefit, offers a big social payoff. Sheep are the very emblems of peace. If we're worried, as the old saw goes, counting imagined sheep will settle our minds enough to sleep. A flock of sheep grazing along a public greenway can be a way of reminding an agitated urban population of its rural roots, or at least of the reassuring storybooks of childhood.

Mr. Richardson's sheep don't look *exactly* like the fluffy ruminants of storybooks, however. They have hair, not wool, and they shed their coats in warm weather, so they don't need to be sheared. They are, in other words, ideally suited for the heat and humidity of the American South, and for grazing an overgrown urban landscape.

When the Chew Crew is hired to clear out a site, Mr. Richardson installs temporary fencing, both to protect the sheep from predators and to protect beneficial vegetation from the sheep, and then he delivers an appropriate-size flock for the site. The sheep do the rest.

Well, not quite *all* the rest. Urban shepherds, like the shepherds of old, must be alert for dangers to the flock: illness, injury, parasites, difficult deliveries. One recent morning Mr. Richardson arrived at Bell's Bend Park, where his pregnant ewes were pastured during lambing season, and found a newborn lamb outside the fence. He picked it up and carried it to each newly delivered ewe in turn, but they all rejected it.

Then he noticed a big ewe in labor. "The lamb was already dead, but it was stuck," he says. "I had to go back to the truck, put the little lost lamb down, get gloves and lubricant and go back to pull the stillborn lamb out. Then I went back to the truck, got the little lost one, rubbed it with the afterbirth and placenta, and nudged it up to the ewe. She looked down at the baby and smelled it, and smelled her own scent, and took it immediately. For a shepherd . . ." He paused. "It was magical."

So how does a city boy like Zach Richardson become a shepherd? It began as a lark in college, when he and his roommates bought some goats to clear their backyard. "They ate everything and turned it from a jungle to a putting green," he says. "It was a huge hit. Everyone wanted to come and sit on our porch." To a student of sustainable landscape architecture, it seemed almost like cheating: the goats had cleared the landscape, improved the ecology, and enriched the human community—and all without chemicals or fuel-guzzling machinery.

Mr. Richardson, whose company T-shirt reads, "Make America Graze Again!" runs the Nashville Chew Crew with the help of one human employee and several canine colleagues. Guard dogs Reba, Sturgill, Dolly, and Dwight are Anatolian shepherds who were born in the company of sheep and who treat the sheep as packmates, living with them day and night, in all seasons and in all weather, to protect them from predators.

Duggie, a Border collie, is a highly trained sheepherding dog whom Mr. Richardson calls his best friend. After finishing his master's degree in 2014, Mr. Richardson went to work for Brian Cash, an urban shepherd in Atlanta who trains sheepdogs in addition to running a flock of sheep for sustainable vegetation management. "He's a world-class handler, breeder, and trainer, and I soaked up as much knowledge as I could from him," Mr. Richardson says. "I traded my first paycheck for Duggie." It's Duggie's job to round up the sheep and herd them safely onto a trailer by following commands from Mr. Richardson.

The Nashville Chew Crew is part of a growing "targeted grazing" movement in the United States, Great Britain, continental Europe, and Canada. This is particularly true in fire-prone areas in the western US. When ruminants like sheep and goats remove the understory while it's still green, before it can dry out and turn into tinder, they create an effective firebreak.

Here in Nashville, Mr. Richardson's sheep can most often be found working the vegetation surrounding the city's public greenways, where they have a near-constant audience: walkers and bikers and businesspeople, even boaters on the Cumberland River, all entranced by the sight of sheep doing what sheep have done for centuries. "Part of why my business is so successful is that we have gotten totally detached from agriculture—babies being born, animals dying, sheep eating foliage," Mr. Richardson says. "People *should* be seeing this—they *should* see a dog work; they *should* see a shepherd who cares about his animals. When I show up with a hundred sheep and some dogs, their eyes light up."

That interest, he believes, can become the catalyst for a greater concern for the environment itself. Even urban landscapes are teeming with wildlife, but most people are too busy to notice. A flock of sheep working a city riverbank can shift their field of vision, expand their gaze. "When you put sheep into an urban landscape, it can be just enough of a spark to get people outside to see something that takes their interest further," Mr. Richardson says. "I see that everywhere we go."

THE MISUNDERSTOOD, MALIGNED RATTLESNAKE

The beautiful creature in the flower bed
was not a threat to us. It was a gift.

JUNE 22, 2020

T he cabin my husband and I borrowed last week was first built in Kentucky on our friends' family land more than a hundred years ago. The timbers are rough-hewed, and you can still see the bark on some of the beams—the builders conserved every inch of the trees, though to them the forest must have seemed endless. Our friends dismantled the cabin in 1987 and brought the timbers back to Tennessee, where they built a new cabin on the Cumberland Plateau. It is now perched at the edge of a windswept bluff overlooking Lost Cove, one of the most biodiverse places in the world, right where the heavens come together with the earth.

In the five days we spent there to celebrate our anniversary, we walked in an endless garden—Queen Anne's lace and forest tickseed, Carolina horse nettle and narrowleaf vervain, annual fleabane and zigzag spiderwort and oxeye daisies were all growing untended on the side of the road. The woods were filled with songbirds: blue jays and goldfinches and tufted titmice and chickadees and bluebirds and even the secretive scarlet tanager. Tanagers generally keep to the treetops, but the trees growing in the soil of Lost Cove reach up to the edge of the bluff. From our own perch, we had a bird's-eye view of the trees.

We watched a pair of red-tailed hawks teaching their fledglings to hunt. We listened to a pileated woodpecker's wild cry from the top of a dead tree and heard a red fox barking in the dark as two barred owls called to each other: *Who, who, who cooks for you?* At Lost Cove, the nights are as beautiful as the days. The fireflies come out to fill the forest just as the stars come out to fill the skies.

The sound that woke me in the first stirrings of dawn one morning was the cry of a small animal—a mouse, perhaps, or a chipmunk—in the claws, or jaws, of a predator. It was a piteous sound that came from directly beneath our window. The creature cried out, just once, and then was silent.

I've mostly made peace with the fact that the peaceable kingdom is anything but. All day long and all night long, too, every creature on that bluff, like every creature deep in the cove itself and every creature in my suburban yard in Nashville and every creature scurrying down every city alleyway, is both trying to eat and trying not to be eaten. An insect-eating scarlet tanager is not inherently less violent than the owl that eats songbirds. A rabbit is not somehow "better" for eating wildflowers than a fox is for eating rabbits. This is how the natural world works, and there is no wishing it were otherwise. But knowing about such suffering is not the same as being a witness to such suffering, and I did not go back to sleep that early morning.

My ambivalence in this matter of mortality explains why I was both completely fascinated and completely terrified by the juvenile rattlesnake my husband found curled up next to the front porch of the cabin later that day. I was afraid, but I wasn't only afraid. I was also a little bit in love with the magnificent creature calmly surveying us from behind a laurel, making not a sound.

Really, what thirty-second wedding anniversary would be complete without the appearance of some perfectly timed memento mori—in this case, a deadly pit viper? Or without an ensuing marital debate?

"It has to be a copperhead," my husband said. "They're all over the place up here. Rattlesnakes are rare."

"The markings are all wrong," I said. "It has to be a timber rattler."

"It's way too small to be a timber rattler," my husband said.

"Rattlesnakes don't start out five feet long," I said.

Throughout this lengthy conversation, which I have truncated for the sake of your sanity, the snake in question did not stir. It was utterly motionless, so still it provided what my husband believed was unassailable evidence of his point: "If this is a rattlesnake, why isn't it rattling?"

A former student settled the question after my husband texted him a picture of the snake. Jackson Roberts is now a doctoral candidate in herpetology at Louisiana State University, and he confirmed that we had in fact been visited by a young timber rattlesnake. "You were really lucky to get to see one," he told us. "They're very shy, and they're becoming more rare as we clear out their habitat. And as people kill them."

I asked Mr. Roberts why the snake hadn't deployed its trademark warning device. "The rattle is a last-ditch defensive strategy against predators," he said. "They'd much rather hunker down and wait for trouble to leave."

To a rattlesnake, in other words, we are the trouble. We are the predators.

Timber rattlesnakes are declining in many states, including here in Tennessee, and it's illegal to kill one. It's actually illegal to kill any snake in Tennessee unless it poses a direct threat to you. Thing is, snakes don't ever directly threaten human beings. Unless you're the one posing a direct threat to the snake—if, say, you step on it, or you're trying to kill it—a snake will simply sit quietly and wait for you to go away.

Barely two days after this peaceful rattlesnake entered my ken and installed itself in my dreams, the Orianne Society, a conservation nonprofit based in Tiger, Georgia, started a new initiative to celebrate rattlesnakes. Every day of the month leading up to World Snake Day on July 16, Orianne is posting clips on social media of chief executive Chris Jenkins talking about snake biology, safe hiking in rattlesnake country, what to do when you encounter a snake—basically anything that might encourage people to stop killing snakes.

"Rattlesnakes, and snakes in general, are the most misunderstood, the most maligned, the most persecuted animals on the planet," Dr. Jenkins said in a phone interview last week. "One of the most important things we can do for the conservation of any snake, and rattlesnakes in particular, is education."

A fear of rattlesnakes is not entirely unfounded. My first cousins' maternal grandfather died decades ago, after he stepped on a rattlesnake too far out in the woods to get medical help quickly. To the snake, he was a threat. To his family, that didn't matter. The only thing that mattered to them was that he was dead.

But the truth is that an animal can be dangerous and still pose almost no threat to people. According to Dr. Jenkins, snakebites are rare, and up to 50 percent of rattlesnake strikes are "dry bites" in which the snake doesn't actually inject venom. Nevertheless, our culture has taught us to associate serpents not only with danger but also with evil.

The only antidote to these associations is information. "Unless you're actively trying to catch or kill a rattlesnake, the chance of being bitten is very low," said Dr. Jenkins. "Many more people die every year from horses—whether they get thrown off or they get kicked—than from snakes. Many more people die from bees and wasps. If you encounter a rattlesnake, you should be excited. It's a symbol that you're in a wild place, a special place."

It's hard to imagine a time when rattlesnakes, no matter how shy and how peaceful, will be welcomed without fear. But I like to think we can still "complicate our perceptions," as my friend Erica Wright writes in her book *Snake*. Perhaps we can yet learn, as she puts it, to "recognize the grace alongside the fangs and venom. Complicated. Sublime. Awful and beautiful together."

When we checked in the last light of day, our rattlesnake visitor was still resting quietly in the flower bed. By morning it was gone, vanished into the dappled forest or the shady crevice of that ancient limestone bluff. We never saw it again.

MAKING WAY FOR MONARCHS

A new wildflower meadow at a Tennessee welcome center is just one of many efforts to address the loss of pollinator habitat.

SEPTEMBER 16, 2019

A few years ago I started noticing wildflowers blooming beside the highway: ironweed and goldenrod and snakeroot and black-eyed Susan. The first time it happened the sun was in my eyes as I drove west toward Memphis, and a late-summer drought was filling the air with dust motes. For a moment I thought I was imagining flowers where flowers had never been before. A daydream on a lonesome stretch of highway as twilight came on.

There was nothing unusual about the flowers themselves—they're the plants that commonly bloom along Nashville's greenways during late summer—but these flowers weren't in a park or a nature preserve. They were growing right on the interstate median and on the side of the road. I figured the Tennessee Department of Transportation simply hadn't gotten around to mowing yet.

Then I started to see the flowers in springtime, too, and all summer. The decision not to mow, it turns out, was deliberate. The Tennessee Department of Transportation—like many other state transportation departments across the country—now practices swath mowing, a strategy that allows wildflowers to bloom unmolested in rural areas till after the first frost. Instead of clearing the entire space between the

41

road and the right-of-way fence, mowers clear only a sixteen-foot-wide area next to the road.

The mowed swath preserves clear sight lines for drivers while allowing wildflowers to grow in the deep margins between the mowed area and the fence. After the wild-flowers have gone to seed, and the seeds have had time to ripen and drop, mowers clear the entire area again to keep trees from becoming established too close to the road. In Tennessee, this plan began as an experimental program in 2013 and now encompasses all rural highways man-aged by the state. That's 13,807 miles of blooming flowers across Tennessee.

The flowers are beautiful, and there's a practical bene-fit to the plan, too: reducing the frequency of mowing saves money. But neither beauty nor cost-cutting is the primary motive for swath mowing. The real reason behind the change is a concern for the health of the state's pollinators—butter-flies, honeybees, native bees, beetles, and other insects.

"We pay attention," said Shawn Bible, manager of the transportation department's Highway Beautification Office. "We knew there was a problem with pollinators, and we saw an opportunity to help, so we jumped in to do it."

Wildflowers once grew in profusion on roadsides every-where. The shoulder of a highway, from blacktop to tree line, is the perfect setting for flowers that require full sun; it's a ribbon of meadow that unfolds before the eye for as long as the road goes on. During my childhood in Alabama, every highway and back road was alight with butterfly weed, which belongs to the family of milkweeds. In summer it formed a bright corridor of orange flowers so covered with orange monarch butterflies that from a distance it looked as though the flowers themselves were taking flight and floating on the breeze.

But the monarch butterfly population has fallen precip-
itously since then. There are many reasons for the drop in
their numbers, including climate change and deforestation
in their Mexican wintering grounds. In this country the
butterfly's greatest threat is habitat destruction along their
migration routes—the loss of both nectar flowers for food
and milkweed plants for reproduction—primarily through
the widespread use of herbicides like Roundup.

In 1996, the year before Roundup-resistant crops were
first planted in the United States, the eastern population of
the migratory monarch butterfly was around seven hundred
million. Since then their numbers have dropped by more than
80 percent, according to the Xerces Society for Invertebrate
Conservation, which works to preserve pollinator populations, and the tally is far worse for the migratory population
west of the Rockies. Down by more than 99 percent, it's now
on the brink of extinction.

But it's not just monarchs. As Ms. Bible noted, other crucial
pollinators are in steep decline worldwide, with about 40
percent of insect pollinators now facing extinction, according to
the Food and Agriculture Organization of the United Nations.

The transformation of American roadsides from narrow
flowering meadows to close-cropped lawns isn't the chief
danger to troubled pollinators, but it hasn't helped. And
unlike the question of how farmers can limit the use of herbicides and still make money, the question of how to restore
roadside meadows so that blooming plants can feed and
sustain pollinators isn't controversial.

Over the years, we've come to expect unvaried green
space to unfold beside us as we drive on interstate highways,
but that expectation is changing. The Tennessee Department
of Transportation was an early adopter of pollinator-friendly

practices, but it's not alone. The Transportation FAST Act, signed into law in December 2015, urged state transportation departments to use land-management practices that promote pollinators.

"Roadsides can offer feeding, breeding, and nesting opportunities for pollinators, and also can aid pollinator migration by linking fragmented habitats and forming habitat corridors," wrote Deirdre Remley and Allison Redmon in *Public Roads*, a publication of the Federal Highway Administration. "Roadsides extend through all types of landscapes and can be particularly important sources of habitat in highly altered landscapes such as intensely managed agricultural lands or urban areas."

Coming home from Alabama this month, I stopped at the Tennessee welcome center in Ardmore, stepped out of my car, and was astonished to discover a newly planted pollinator meadow just down the hill. Up close, the acre-size plot was blooming with asters and liatris and ironweed and two different kinds of goldenrod. The plot was so loud with insects that the roar of highway traffic, only yards away up the little hill, was faint by comparison. While I stood there, dumbfounded, a monarch butterfly floated past. I was too stunned to take its picture.

The Ardmore rest area is the first meadow that the transportation department has specifically planted for pollinators, but others are in the works, among other pollinator-friendly initiatives. The department announced a new partnership with the Tennessee Department of Environment and Conservation and the Tennessee Department of Agriculture to promote pollinators in state parks by planting wildflower meadows within park borders.

In Ardmore, just behind the fence beyond the pollinator meadow, is more state property. It is not planted or managed, and yet it, too, is blooming with ironweed and goldenrod and snakeroot. Last week, I asked Ms. Bible about it. "That's one of those wonderful opportunities" to let nature set the agenda, she said. "Those plantings are just natural."

THE CALL OF THE AMERICAN
LOTUS

*Heaven is the Mobile-Tensaw Delta when
its mythical flower is in bloom.*

JULY 9, 2018

F rom the middle of its namesake delta, the city of Mobile, Alabama, looks like a mythical place: shiny skyscrapers framed by cattails and marsh grass, a city that reaches into a sky so vast it seems to hold all the weather there is— bright sun and cottony clouds and pregnant thunderheads and torrential rain—all at one time. From the middle of that magnificent delta, Mobile could be Atlantis rising from the sea or the Emerald City of Oz.

Weather is unpredictable on the Alabama coast in summertime. In February, when we planned this trip, my husband and I were hoping to arrive on a day that offered at least one two-hour window of clear skies, just long enough to get out on the Mobile-Tensaw Delta in Jimbo Meador's flat-bottomed boat and see the American lotuses in bloom. By the time we actually arrived in mid-June, the forecast called for intermittent storms.

Standing next to his boat in a slip near the Bluegill, a restaurant on the Battleship Parkway in Spanish Fort, Mr. Meador was studying his phone, toggling between weather apps. Each showed squalls arriving in an unpredictable pattern all day. "Let's go on out," he said. "Worst thing that could happen is we get struck by lightning in a beautiful place."

He was joking, but the Mobile-Tensaw Delta is in fact an indescribably beautiful place. Encompassing roughly three hundred square miles, it is the second-largest delta region in the United States, trailing only the far more famous Mississippi Delta. The Mobile-Tensaw watershed is fed by nine rivers carrying water from much of Alabama, as well as parts of Mississippi and Georgia. Its estuary ecosystem includes open water, marsh, swamp, and bottomland hardwood forests. It serves as a home to some sixty-seven rare species, many threatened or endangered. Designated a National Natural Landmark, it is also an important way station for migrating songbirds.

I knew all that because I took this tour two years ago. Mr. Meador's encyclopedic knowledge of the delta—its history, its ecology, its creatures, and its flowers—is how I first heard about the flower I have come to see. The American lotus is a creamy yellow flower the size of a luncheon plate that rises above floating pads of foliage so large they collect rainwater. His description of those watery fields of gently swaying flowers opening to the infinite delta sky, which I had missed on that first trip, is what made me want to come back.

In 1976, my eighth-grade English class read Edith Hamilton's *Mythology*. On the back cover, in someone else's fourteen-year-old handwriting, are the words "This book is boring." I, on the other hand, loved that book, and I've held on to my copy all these years. In her summary of *The Odyssey*, Ms. Hamilton describes the Lotus Eaters, who shared their "flower food" with Odysseus's sailors: "Those who tasted it . . . lost their longing for home," she writes. Odysseus had to capture his sailors and chain them to the ship. "They wept, so great was their desire to stay, tasting forever the honey-sweet flowers."

47

For a certain kind of child, the prospect of seeing such flowers can become something of an obsession, even across decades, and Jimbo Meador, seventy-seven years old, is the kind of boatman who understands an obsession like that. A certified master naturalist, he has spent most of his life in this maze of a delta, where the water and the land come together with the sky.

He is locally famous for catching unwelcome alligators with his bare hands and relocating them to safer environs, but he is also a literary man who has written for magazines and counts among his friends writers like Jim Harrison and Thomas McGuane, who dedicated *Live Water* to him. The novelist Winston Groom is a lifelong friend—*Forrest Gump* is also dedicated to Jimbo (along with another childhood friend, George Radcliff). When the film version of *Forrest Gump* was released in 1994, rumors flew that Mr. Groom's protagonist was based on Jimbo Meador, a onetime passionate runner who knows a lot about shrimp. What's true is that a dialect coach from Paramount did go down to Alabama to record Mr. Meador's voice so Tom Hanks could emulate his accent.

Hearing Mr. Meador tell a story is one of the chief pleasures of his ecotours of the Mobile-Tensaw Delta, and he has a huge array of stories to draw from, depending on his visitors' interests. Many people get on his boat hoping to see birds—more than three hundred species have been identified in the delta—and Mr. Meador knows them all by sight and most by song. Other people want to learn about the delta's history: the daily life of the Creeks, who lived there first; the last major battle of the Civil War, which was fought at Fort Blakely at the edge of the delta ("Lee had actually surrendered, but they didn't get the email," Mr. Meador said);

a "ghost fleet" of World War II Liberty ships anchored for decades in the fresh water of the Tensaw River to keep them safe from corrosion in case they were needed again.

But Mr. Meador's chief aim is to educate people about the ecological necessity of this delta. "Nitrogen and phosphorus runoff is what's causing these algae blooms in the Gulf," he said. "It used to be the ground absorbed the rain. Now everything is paved and roofed, and it runs off into the tributaries and straight into the rivers without getting filtered out. But all the plant life in this delta utilizes the nitrogen and phosphorus that's running down all these rivers, so it acts as a huge filter. Nature's pretty good at taking care of itself if we let it."

In an interview with Ben Raines of the Mobile *Press-Register*, biologist and environmental activist E. O. Wilson, who also spent much of his childhood in the area, calls the Mobile-Tensaw Delta "arguably the biologically richest place" Americans have: "It has more species of plants and animals than any comparable area anywhere in North America, the United States and Canada."

On the way to the lotuses, Mr. Meador took care to point out an enormous variety of birds and flowers. We saw brown pelicans and ospreys (including two active nests), laughing gulls, marsh hens (one with newly hatched chicks), Caspian terns, eastern kingbirds, anhingas, belted kingfishers, one purple gallinule, two species of egret and three species of heron—and we weren't even looking for birds. We saw morning glory, alligator weed, water hemlock, arrow arum, elderberry flowers, black needlerush, rose mallow, and scores of other wildflowers, all as interesting as the mythical flowers we came to see.

But, oh, the flowers we came to see! The American lotus is no relation to those in Homer's epic, but it is every

49

bit as intoxicating as the ancient lotus of yore: thousands of pale-yellow flowers rising on foot-high stalks above floating pads with water pearled across their surfaces, the petals of each bloom curling gently toward the sun. Their deep-golden centers are tangled with white-tipped stamens, a flower within a flower, and their enormous, unopened buds are as delicately furled as any miniature rose.

There was not another human soul in sight, and Mr. Meador cut his boat's motor. The only sounds were birdsong and lapping water and the buzz of lotus-drunk bees gathering pollen from the feast spread out before them. It was an alien landscape to me, far from my childhood in the red-dirt pineywoods of rural Alabama, farther still from my life today in the suburbs of Nashville, but for just a few moments I felt I belonged there. For a few timeless moments, my face inches from an American lotus in full bloom, I forgot myself. Just for an instant, I lost my longing for home.

POLITICS
& RELIGION

A MONUMENT THE OLD
SOUTH WOULD LIKE
TO IGNORE

*The debate over the fate of Nashville's Fort Negley tests the
traditional Southern argument for preserving history.*

JANUARY 29, 2018

In 1978, the city of Nashville leased eighteen acres of a
Civil War monument to a local businessman who wanted
to start a new baseball franchise—the Nashville Sounds,
then a Double A expansion team for the Southern League—
and needed a place for his team to play. It was a ludicrous
arrangement from the start: a privately owned ball field built
on public land.

And not just any public land. Greer Stadium was built
at the base of St. Cloud Hill, where the Union Army erected
a stronghold after taking control of the city in 1862. Fort
Negley was an investment designed to protect the Union's
hold on Nashville and its strategic access to roads, railroad
lines, and the Cumberland River.

Fort Negley Park is not a Civil War monument in the
South that celebrates the heroism of the Confederacy, in
other words. Fort Negley Park is a Civil War monument
in the South that celebrates the preservation of the United
States of America. The question of what will happen to it has
roiled Nashville for more than a year.

In part, that's because it's a crucial site for Black history
as well. During the war, the grounds surrounding Fort Negley

served as a de facto refugee camp for escaped slaves. In an irony lost on no one today, the Union Army immediately forced those refugees into service; under brutal conditions, some twenty-seven hundred of them built Fort Negley itself. Many lost their lives and are believed to be buried at Fort Negley Park. When the South surrendered, the survivors—joined by other freed slaves—settled in the area. Today the area is gentrifying, home to new art galleries and coffee shops, but it is still populated largely by lower-income African Americans.

In their midst now lies one badly overgrown and dilapidated minor-league ball field. Greer Stadium has sat empty since the Nashville Sounds departed at the end of the 2014 season. As part of a preserved Civil War site, the stadium's location has long been designated as public parkland, going back to 1928, when the city purchased it from the descendants of John Overton, a crony of President Andrew Jackson. That parcel was always meant to revert to parkland once the Sounds decamped.

The actual fort at Fort Negley Park was dismantled after the Union Army withdrew in 1867, but history set its hand on the site a second time during the Great Depression, when a facsimile of the fort was built by eight hundred laborers funded by the Works Progress Administration. That reproduction ultimately fell into ruin and for decades was closed to the public, but 1996 brought a plan to restore the site again. Fort Negley reopened in 2004, on the 140th anniversary of the Battle of Nashville. The next year it was designated a local Historic Landmark District.

Three years after the Sounds left, Mayor Megan Barry released a request for proposals related to the site of the old stadium. The request was not for Metro Parks to create a plan for desperately needed green space in an already overpaved urban core. The request was not for the Metropolitan Historical Commission to create a plan to preserve the legacy of African Americans who gave their lives to preserve the Union. It was not a request for the Friends of Fort Negley, an advocacy group, to create a plan to expand the educational reach of the site.

The plans the mayor requested were for private development under a land-lease arrangement much like the one that allowed Greer Stadium to be built there in the first place.

Let's call what happened next the second Battle of Nashville.

For years this city has been undergoing rapid, unchecked growth, and it desperately needs affordable housing and subsidized work spaces for artists and innovators. That much everyone agrees on. When the mayor's office approved a plan by the Cloud Hill partnership, headed by the developer Bert Mathews and the music producer T Bone Burnett, for a mixed-use private development that would include music and art studios, retail space, and housing at three price points—affordable, workforce, and market rate—it made a kind of sense.

But an army of green-space advocates and historic preservationists quickly mobilized to point out what would seem to be obvious: Nashville owns a lot of land, and there is no good reason to allow for-profit development on a park with huge historic significance.

For an entire year, Betsy Phillips, a local historian, published article after article in the *Nashville Scene*, looking at every possible angle for understanding the importance of Fort Negley, particularly its significance to African American history. The bottom line, she wrote in December, is that we preserve historic sites for future generations because "we don't know what the future might need from the past."

The best-selling historical novelist Robert Hicks, an advocate for preserving Civil War historic sites, entered the fray. A Nashville council member sued Metro government, arguing that the mayor's office didn't follow city rules in granting the development contract. The country music legend Kix Brooks took to Facebook to plead for preserving the integrity of the park. Historic Nashville, Inc., a nonprofit that each year releases a list of the nine most endangered historical sites in the city, took the unprecedented step in 2017 of naming only one: Fort Negley.

The Friends of Fort Negley, led by historian Clay Bailey, took a multipronged approach to raising the site's national profile. It petitioned the Tennessee Historical Commission to designate Fort Negley Park a "historical memorial," a label that under state law means a site cannot be altered without a waiver from the commission itself. With help from Nashville's NAACP chapter, it submitted a proposal for Fort Negley to be included on UNESCO's slave route registry—the first United States site to be nominated for this international recognition.

The group produced a website and a video summarizing the issues for a public that was finally tuning in: in its annual Landslide report, the Cultural Landscape Foundation in Washington recognized Fort Negley as one of thirteen nationally significant landscapes in need of protection.

And all this was happening against the backdrop of a national debate about Civil War monuments. Defenders of monuments to Robert E. Lee and Nathan Bedford Forrest, the Confederate generals most often at the heart of these contentions, are fond of pointing out that such statues weren't erected to celebrate the institution of slavery; they were erected to celebrate Southern history. The anti-monument contingent rolls its eyes at this argument: if not for antislavery sentiment in the North, the South would never have seceded.

It's important to note that Southern attitudes to Civil War monuments are not uniform, though the pro-con divide typically follows the rural-urban divide.

In 2015, Nashville's Metro Council voted to petition the Tennessee Department of Transportation to plant obscuring vegetation in front of a truly hideous statue of Nathan Bedford Forrest on I-65. The giant statue is visible from the highway to anyone entering the city from the south, but it stands on private land, and for that reason the department declined to intervene. Never mind that the TDOT itself removed obscuring vegetation back in 1998, when the statue was first erected. Last month, activists took matters into their own hands and painted the statue pussy-hat pink.

The Tennessee Heritage Protection Act was passed in 2013 and updated in 2016 with what seemed to be an express intent to prevent municipalities in Tennessee from taking down Confederate memorials. (Yes, this is the same act currently being invoked to protect Fort Negley.) Leaders in Memphis found a novel way around the state's intrusion into municipal decisions: they sold two city parks to a nonprofit. Within hours of the sale, statues of Nathan Bedford Forrest and Jefferson Davis had been removed.

On January 12, back in Nashville, the development controversy finally came to a close when an archaeological survey commissioned by the city found it "highly likely" that former slaves are still buried there. Cloud Hill formally withdrew its development proposal, and it's not clear what will happen to the Greer parcel now. Nashville's 2018 parks budget does not include funding for bulldozing Greer Stadium and returning it to parkland, but Mayor Barry recently acknowledged that the presence of graves changes the way the old baseball stadium should be approached.

"The likelihood of graves means that we should reassess plans for this site so as to better honor and preserve the history of the men and women who died in the construction of a fort that helped save the Union," she wrote in a statement. "As we move forward, I want to see that whatever happens with the Greer Stadium site will honor that history, while bringing the community together around a shared vision. I have faith in the ability of all stakeholders to work together to identify and coalesce around this vision."

It's fair to assume that the supporters of other Civil War monuments around the state of Tennessee will not be coalescing around this vision to preserve a site that celebrates a different kind of history, but the Friends of Fort Negley is moving ahead with plans of its own. Last Thursday it announced that Kix Brooks will serve on a new committee. Its goal: to unite Nashville around a plan—and funding—for a reunified Fort Negley Park.

THE HITS KEEP COMING
FOR THE RED-STATE POOR

Following the Koch playbook, Tennessee keeps finding
new ways to undermine the welfare of its citizens.

MARCH 18, 2019

The 111th General Assembly of Tennessee convened on January 8, and it will disperse on April 26, not a moment too soon. Already, its Republican supermajority has introduced bills that would further weaken lax gun laws, increase campaign-donation limits, and undermine a progressive Nashville law passed by public referendum, among other assaults on democracy and good sense. Tennesseans should get down on their knees and thank God for the citizen-legislator model of government, because there's no telling how much damage these people could do if they met all year.

So far this year, Tennessee Republicans have introduced bills to amend the state constitution (they want it to insist that "liberties do not come from government, but from Almighty God"), prohibit state officials from recognizing marriages between people of the same gender, deny birth certificates to babies born to undocumented parents, and, most controversially, outlaw abortion after a fetal heartbeat can be detected. Heart cells begin beating so early in gestation that many women don't yet know they're pregnant.

None of these proposed laws would accomplish anything. God is already invoked three times in the constitution of Tennessee, and the United States Constitution has already established birthright citizenship for babies born in this country. The Supreme Court has made same-sex marriage the law of the land, and the "heartbeat bill" would run afoul of *Roe v. Wade*, the landmark Supreme Court ruling that protects a woman's right to an abortion. The American Civil Liberties Union of Tennessee and Planned Parenthood of Tennessee and North Mississippi have already announced that they will challenge the law if it's passed, and they will win in court.

Bills like this are red meat to the constituencies that elected the Republican supermajority in the first place. But this year, resistance to their efforts has come from surprising places: business and the religious right.

Last May the asset-management firm AllianceBernstein announced that it would be moving its headquarters to Nashville—and creating more than a thousand jobs here—in part because of $17.5 million in financial incentives provided by the state. Earlier this month, the company's chief executive, James Gingrich, joined with local LGBTQ advocates in assailing several bills designed to suppress gay rights in Tennessee, pointing out that such bills in other states have proven to be "anti-growth, anti-job and against the interests of the citizens of those states."

The fetal-heartbeat bill faces similar opposition from within a traditional Republican camp. All three of Tennessee's Catholic bishops oppose the bill, and so does Tennessee Right to Life, the primary antiabortion group in the state. That's because a losing court battle would force the state to pay costly legal fees—its own and its opponents'—as well as create a legal precedent that would dog future antiabortion efforts. The Tennessee House of Representatives passed the bill on a 65-21 vote.

It now goes to the state Senate for consideration.

It would be easy to dismiss, even laugh at, politicians so resolutely determined to shoot themselves in the foot. But from time to time they do manage to pass laws, and some of those laws cause immense pain to innocent people. In 2015, members of the Republican supermajority rejected a plan by their own Republican governor, Bill Haslam, to expand TennCare, the state's Medicaid program, and provide health insurance to hundreds of thousands of low-income Tennesseans not covered by the Affordable Care Act. Governor Haslam's plan would have cost the state no additional funds, and it was supported by an overwhelming majority of Tennesseans. Adding insult to injury, the failure to expand Medicaid has caused the widespread closure of hospitals in this state—a dozen so far, with many others teetering on the verge of insolvency—and there have been many other predictable ramifications of leaving so many people without health insurance.

In 2018, the state legislature passed a law that required "able-bodied" Tennesseans who do qualify for TennCare to hold a job or go to school if they want to keep their health insurance. The state is currently seeking permission from the federal government to implement this requirement and will presumably get it. When that happens, sixty-eight thousand more Tennesseans will lose their health insurance—because they lack transportation, for example, or don't have access to affordable or reliable childcare. The requirements will also cost the state an additional $19 million in administrative costs, even taking into account the money saved by reducing TennCare rolls. Republican lawmakers may not be concerned about their uninsured fellow citizens, but you'd think a figure like that might catch their attention.

Every morning I read Joel Ebert's heroic statehouse reporting for *The Tennessean*, Nashville's daily newspaper, and I wonder what in the world is going on. These are not stupid people. What possible explanation lies behind such stupid behavior?

Lately, though, I've been remembering the Duke University historian Nancy MacLean's brilliant book, *Democracy in Chains: The Deep History of the Radical Right's Stealth Plan for America*. The book is a history of a decades-long effort by the far right—a network of wealthy political donors organized by brothers Charles G. and David H. Koch—to take over statehouse governments and enact an extreme libertarian agenda at the local level. The irrational behavior of the Tennessee General Assembly is completely coherent when viewed through the book's lens.

According to Dr. MacLean, the Koch network's goal— and the goal of all legislators in thrall to the Kochs' PACs—is to weaken unions, suppress voter turnout, privatize public education, undercut climate science, roll back existing environmental protections, dismantle the social safety net, and stack the courts with sympathetic judges. To enact that unpopular agenda, they've had to make common cause with the religious right.

Indeed, virtually every bill introduced in Tennessee's General Assembly this legislative session is designed to out-right the religious right (by, for example, introducing an antiabortion bill that can't possibly survive legal scrutiny), diminish the legislative power of blue cities, and, above all, demonize anyone who can be painted as a needy "other."

We tend to focus our shock and outrage on the manifold travesties unfolding on the national stage, but it's a mistake to tune out what's happening in statehouses around the country, for Tennessee is far from unique in following the Koch playbook. Hours after Tennessee legislators passed the fetal-heartbeat bill, Georgia passed a nearly identical one, and in recent years similar bills have passed in Arkansas, Florida, Iowa, Kentucky, Minnesota, Mississippi, Missouri, North Dakota, and Ohio. Fifteen other states have added work requirements of some kind for Medicaid. Texas has already tried, and failed, to prevent the children born to undocumented parents from receiving birth certificates. It's the death of compassionate democracy by a thousand paper cuts.

Dr. MacLean notes that even Justice Clarence Thomas, one of the most conservative members of the Supreme Court, has expressed profound concern about the current state of the body politic: "We are going to have to recognize that we are destroying our institutions," he said in a conversation she quotes in *Democracy in Chains*. He was talking to the Heritage Foundation, a conservative think tank. For all its often-empty swagger, the Tennessee General Assembly has made one thing clear: if Americans don't start paying closer attention to what's happening in statehouses across the country, the republic may never recover.

LIES, DAMN LIES, AND GEORGIA

*The election of Raphael Warnock and Jon Ossoff is a
clear message: the South is truly changing.*

JANUARY 11, 2021

I t's impossible not to notice how many members of Congress
who voted to overturn the 2020 presidential election were
white Southerners—more than *half* the legislators who
professed to believe Donald Trump's lie that the election was
stolen are people who represent the American South. Even
after his supporters, egged on by the president himself, staged
a violent insurrection inside the United States Capitol, these
craven, feckless legislators would not vote to certify the results
of an election that has survived the scrutiny of more than sixty
baseless challenges in various courts.

Others, including my own state's two senators, entered
the Senate chamber on January 6 fully intending to join
them but were moved by the violent attack on the Capitol
to reverse course. "These actions at the US Capitol by pro-
testors are truly despicable and unacceptable," tweeted
Marsha Blackburn, a Republican senator from Tennessee.
"I condemn them in the strongest possible terms. We are a
nation of laws."

We are also a nation of free and fair elections, but somehow Ms. Blackburn had managed to ignore that necessary
part of our democratic compact. She was not alone in her
tardy about-face. All across the Southern states, politicians

scrambled to reassert their own faith in the rule of law after publicly flouting it for weeks—or years, depending on when you start counting.

Senator Lindsey Graham, Republican of South Carolina, belatedly recognizing the nature of his own constituency, called the insurrectionists "terrorists, not patriots."

"Violence is abhorrent and I strongly condemn today's attacks on our Capitol," tweeted Senator Kelly Loeffler, Republican of Georgia, who had just spent two months running for reelection while simultaneously joining the president in insisting that the election was rigged.

With such elected "leaders" representing this region— and with the insurrectionists parading through our nation's Capitol carrying Confederate battle flags and other symbols of white supremacy—it's not surprising that so many people outside the South seem to believe that the voters who support Marsha Blackburn, Lindsey Graham, and Kelly Loeffler, not even to mention Donald Trump, are the only people who live here.

All I can say is thank God for Georgia.

In the runoff elections last week, the good people of Georgia sent two Democrats to Washington, DC: the Reverend Dr. Raphael Warnock, the pastor of Ebenezer Baptist Church, where the Reverend Dr. Martin Luther King Jr. once served as a co-pastor, and Jon Ossoff, a Jewish film executive who ran for Senate with the blessing of John Lewis, the civil rights activist and longtime member of Congress who passed away in July. In electing them, Georgia delivered the Senate to Democrats and at the same time offered a clear illustration of something Southerners, liberal and conservative alike, have known for years: the American South is in the midst of profound change.

This is not a story of twenty-first-century carpetbaggers moving to the South to take advantage of our cheap cost of living and then blowing up our long-standing election patterns, an argument I've heard from more than one conservative Southerner.

Partly, as other writers have noted, what is changing in the South is the demographic makeup. Urban and suburban voters, and the residents of college towns, are more apt to be progressive, and that's true whether they're homegrown or new residents. Every red state in the region has them. Think of Memphis and Nashville. Think of Chapel Hill and Birmingham and Louisville and New Orleans and Austin. As small towns dry up and jobs in the countryside disappear, it only stands to reason that these ever-growing cities and their suburbs will eventually loosen the stranglehold that rural voters have always had over elections in the South—at least in statewide elections, where gerrymandered districts don't matter.

But Republicans still hold the power in almost all Southern state legislatures (Virginia's is the exception, and only since 2019), and they will continue to do everything possible to make it harder for Democrats to vote. In Georgia, state legislators are already eyeing new ways to avoid a repeat of the elections that turned Georgia blue. Consequently, change in the South may always be of the two-steps-forward-one-step-back variety.

Which brings us to the other major explanation for why the South is changing: liberals and progressives keep fighting back. Stacey Abrams is the face of this fight, and she is rightly credited with flipping Georgia two years after unapologetic voter-suppression tactics ended her own hopes of serving as governor. But the New Georgia Project, the mighty voter-outreach organization that Ms. Abrams and her colleagues have built to register new voters and persuade long-disenfranchised Black and brown voters not to give up on the democratic process, has analogues across the South. These efforts may be less visible than Ms. Abrams's, and some of them are still embryonic, but they are growing.

That's why Democrats down here haven't completely lost heart, despite consistently losing elections to Republicans on one side and being chastised by liberals outside the South on the other. ("Everyday Democrats need to see beyond the electoral map to acknowledge the folks pushing for liberal ideas even in the reddest of areas," the Kentucky novelist Silas House notes in a new essay for *The Atlantic*. "If they don't, the cultural divide will grow only wider.")

In addition to voting demographics and voter outreach, a small but not inconsequential explanation for the changing political landscape of the South is that Donald Trump has finally inspired a change of heart in plenty of white Southerners. You won't find them waving banners at political rallies or posting diatribes on social media, but they are here.

Many of them sat out the last election, true, but others quietly, bravely cast their votes for Democrats, often for the first time in their lives, because this president has made them see how thin the veneer of democracy really is in today's Republican Party. It isn't easy for them to defy their entire family or their entire church to vote for candidates who stand for fairness and inclusion, but they did it in 2020, and already in 2021, and I believe that their numbers will continue to grow.

I hope you'll remember them, and all the passionate liberal activists here, too, the next time you see a sea of red on an election map. I hope you'll remember them the next time a Southern statehouse passes another law that constrains the rights of LGBTQ citizens or guts public education or makes it harder to choose an abortion but easier to buy a gun. I hope you'll look beyond the headlines to what is also happening here, often at great risk to those who are making it happen. Because Georgia is the clearest proof yet that this is not our grandfather's Southland anymore. And it will never be again.

WE'RE ALL ADDICTS HERE

*With Tennesseans dying every day from opioid overdose,
state Republicans' refusal to expand Medicaid
amounts to an act of cruelty.*

MAY 28, 2018

In 2009, my husband had an emergency spinal-fusion operation to prevent permanent nerve damage caused by a ruptured disk. I was rolling the IV pole while he pushed a walker around the hospital corridor when I got an urgent call from a friend: "Don't let them give him pain pills," she said.

I told her the nurses were giving him oxycodone on a schedule because the drug works better to prevent pain than to knock it back once it's out of control. She was insistent: "Well, get him off it as fast as you can when you get home. Mom was addicted within a week of her back surgery, and she's been addicted ever since. We can't get her off it."

I knew my friend's mother, and I had no idea she was addicted to painkillers. I'd never even heard of an addiction to prescription drugs. To me, a "drug addict" was a desperate person who bought illegal drugs on the street. An addict was not an elderly woman who'd gone to a reputable surgeon and taken the medication he'd prescribed exactly as he'd prescribed it.

My friend's mother is dead now, and rampant opioid addiction is something no one can ignore anymore. In 1999, 342 Tennesseans died of an opioid overdose, according to

69

an investigative report from *The Tennessean* earlier this year. By 2009, the year my husband had his back operation, that number was up to 430, an increase of not quite 26 percent in ten years.

Since then, the numbers have surged. In 2016, the most recent year for which figures are available, 1,631 Tennesseans died of an opioid overdose, an increase of 279 percent in seven years.

In spite of such appalling numbers, Tennessee still ranks second highest in the nation in opioid prescriptions—"more than one prescription for every man, woman and child" in the state, according to *The Tennessean*. "For every overdose death, the state estimates there are 14 nonfatal overdoses."

Despite being on the leading edge of this epidemic, Tennessee did not create it. This is a national trend. "Drug overdose deaths in the United States more than tripled from 1999 to 2015," according to a 2017 report by the United States Centers for Disease Control and Prevention. "The current epidemic of drug overdoses began in the 1990s, driven by increasing deaths from prescription opioids that paralleled a dramatic increase in the prescribing of such drugs for chronic pain."

Two weeks ago, Tennessee joined five other states in suing Purdue Pharma, maker of OxyContin, for aggressive marketing practices that included downplaying the drug's risk of addiction and exaggerating its benefits in treating chronic pain. "We believe Purdue's conduct has been unconscionable, and we intend to hold the company accountable," Attorney General Herbert Slatery said in a statement. "Three Tennesseans are dying each day from opioid-related overdoses, and we are committed to the hard work that needs to be done to address this tragedy."

It may seem unusual for the attorney general of a red state to take on Big Pharma, but this lawsuit is only one part of Tennessee's response to the calamity. In January, Governor Bill Haslam, a Republican, proposed a $30 million plan, called TN Together, to address the opioid crisis across the state. The plan, which the Tennessee General Assembly approved last month, limits prescriptions, equips state troopers with Narcan (an emergency treatment for opioid overdose), and funds addiction treatment for Tennesseans who can't afford it otherwise, primarily those who have no health insurance.

But, as is so often the case with Republican public health policies, both the lawsuit and TN Together are too little too late. The $25 million that TN Together earmarks for treatment, for example, will treat 6,000 to 10,000 addicted Tennesseans, according to state estimates, while the number of Tennesseans who actually abused opioids in 2016 was 317,647. And approximately 82,000 of them were already addicted.

In 2015, Governor Haslam tried to persuade the Republican supermajority in the Tennessee General Assembly to expand Medicaid in the state through a federally approved, budget-neutral compromise to the Affordable Care Act. In keeping with a long tradition of defying common sense, statehouse legislators said no. If they had said yes, Tennessee would likely be enjoying addiction news similar to Kentucky's: "After expanding Medicaid," notes the Center on Budget and Policy Priorities, "Kentucky experienced a 700 percent increase in Medicaid beneficiaries using substance-use treatment services." That number coincides with a 90 percent drop in overdose hospitalizations of uninsured Kentuckians.

My senior English course in high school was a survey of British literature. Somewhere toward the middle of the unit on Romantic poets, a boy in my class raised his hand and asked our teacher why so many of the writers we studied were drug addicts and alcoholics. More to the point, he wondered, why should we be reading the work of people who were clearly moral failures?

I don't remember that student's exact words, but I remember our teacher's response. "When someone is struggling with addiction," she said, "remember that you don't know how many times he resisted that temptation before he finally gave in. A person who resists ninety-nine times, even if he gives in the hundredth, is a stronger person than someone who's never been tempted at all."

I have thought of that beloved teacher's words countless times over the past thirty-eight years. It's such decent, human advice: before judging another person, consider all the kinder ways there are to interpret what might seem at first like a terrible moral failing. And the way to do that is to imagine what it feels like to be fighting their battles.

Here in Tennessee, our struggling neighbors won't benefit from federal dollars through Medicaid expansion for the same reason Tennesseans won't benefit from so many other things that citizens of other states can take for granted. Why? Because Republicans in the Tennessee General Assembly are consistently more committed to defying what they see as federal overreach than to helping their own vulnerable citizens.

I don't know what these legislators are thinking. No doubt they believe they're doing the right thing. Still, it looks a lot like a colossal failure of empathy. Maybe they just can't imagine what it feels like to have no medical insurance. Maybe they can't imagine what it feels like to be in chronic pain. Maybe they can't imagine what it feels like to be addicted and to have no hope.

An optimist might call TN Together and the lawsuit against Purdue Pharma the start of meaningful efforts to resolve the opioid crisis. But if that's as far as it goes, if a lot more isn't done to help, it can't be considered a start at all.

THERE IS A MIDDLE GROUND
ON GUNS

Even in gun country, keeping armed people out of
schools is not too much to ask.

April 2, 2018

I didn't attend the local rally against gun violence on March 24, though more than ten thousand Nashvillians did. The march was planned by Abby Brafman, a Vanderbilt University freshman and 2017 graduate of Marjory Stoneman Douglas High School in Parkland, Florida. I had out-of-town family visiting, so my husband, a high school English teacher, marched alone. A few minutes after he got to the rally, he texted me a photo he'd taken of himself standing in front of another marcher's sign. It read "Am I next?" For just a second, I couldn't breathe.

I had a similar reaction last summer when our oldest son, a new middle school math teacher, took me to see his first classroom. "Just look at all these beautiful windows!" I said. "Not exactly great for an active-shooter situation," he pointed out. His words turned my heart to ice.

Not only am I married to a schoolteacher, and the mother of one, I also have two younger sons in college. Not a single day goes by when I don't worry about whether they will all be safe in their classrooms.

Every parent in this country knows we're taking a calculated risk when we send our children to school, to a concert, to a movie. The canned statement that used to make us roll

our eyes at public events—"Please take a moment to famil-
iarize yourself with the location of the exits in the unlikely
event of an emergency"—has become our unconscious habit
because such emergencies are no longer so unthinkable:
Americans are now more likely to be shot to death than to die
in a car accident.

Everyone is worried about the threat of gun violence,
and almost everyone has a clear idea of what to do about
it, too. A new Fox News poll—Fox News!—showed strong
bipartisan support for at least some forms of gun control:
91 percent of Americans support criminal background
checks, 84 percent support mandatory mental health
checks, and 60 percent called for an outright ban on
assault rifles and semiautomatic weapons. "By a 13-point
margin [53 percent to 40 percent], voters consider protecting against gun violence more important than protecting gun rights," Fox reported.

Here in the American South, however, plenty of people
still ardently believe our trouble isn't guns. Americans have
"a heart problem," not a gun problem, the House majority
leader of the Tennessee General Assembly said in March.

This is an easy conclusion to come to if you've grown up
in a culture where guns are ubiquitous. My grandfather, a
farmer, kept his shotgun hanging on hooks over the coatrack
because it was not uncommon for him to need it. My father,
a salesman who often had appointments in crime-ridden
neighborhoods, carried a handgun on nighttime calls and
taught me to shoot it when I was fourteen. It never crossed
their minds that I or anyone else might pick up one of those
guns without a very good reason.

For my father and my grandfather, a gun was a tool. It
was not a toy. They would not have been able to conceive of

a world in which civilians could purchase weapons of war, a culture in which gun-entranced suburbanites could host birthday parties where children fire off AR-15s for fun at a homemade range on someone's family farm.

I will never understand the kind of thinking that makes shooting guns a sport, but that doesn't mean I don't understand why a person in certain circumstances might need to have a gun. In 1982, my grandmother was sitting in a rocking chair just inside the door of a tiny grocery store in rural Alabama when a stranger walked in with a rifle and pointed it at the store owner's head. My grandmother cried out a warning, and the man turned and shot her instead. While the intruder was busy firing five bullets into my seventy-two-year-old grandmother's chest and abdomen, the store owner retrieved his own handgun from beneath the counter and killed him. My grandmother was shot by a bad guy with a gun. She lived another twenty-four years because of the proverbial good guy with a gun.

There is no need for polarities here. Most people who don't own guns understand that some people might truly need to own a gun. Most people who do own guns understand the need to keep other people safe. But our legislators, in thrall to the National Rifle Association, do almost nothing to keep guns away from people who shouldn't have them, or to keep the most dangerous weapons—those meant to inflict the greatest damage to the most people in the least amount of time—out of the hands of civilians.

Tennessee has some of the most permissive gun laws in the country. You don't need a permit to buy a gun here. You don't need a license to own one. You aren't required to register any gun you own. You don't need a permit to carry a rifle or a shotgun. You aren't required to pass a background check if you're buying a gun from a private seller. It's easier to purchase an AR-15 in Tennessee than it is to become a licensed exotic dancer, as two employees of Déjà Vu Showgirls, a Nashville strip club, demonstrated in a recent YouTube video.

Tennessee students are caught bringing a gun to school at twice the rate of the national average. The Tennessee General Assembly's response to this unwelcome trend is to propose arming teachers. If passed, the bill, directed at campuses without a school resource officer, would allow a percentage of teachers to carry a concealed weapon. More than half the members of the Tennessee House of Representatives have cosigned the bill, though it is opposed by state education officials, the teachers' union, the Tennessee Sheriffs' Association, and Governor Bill Haslam, a Republican.

It's never a good bet to look for sane behavior from the Tennessee General Assembly, but the opposition to this bill gives me hope. I don't want my husband to work in a school where teachers are armed. I don't want my son to work in a school where teachers are armed. All I want is for this state—and this country—to keep anyone else from going to school armed.

Judging from the Fox News poll results, this is an opinion nearly all of us share. How remarkable it is, at a time when Americans don't agree on very much, for the response to a terrible problem to be so straightforward and so clear. We don't need to repeal the Second Amendment. We just need to do everything we can to keep guns out of the hands of people who shouldn't have them.

AN AMERICAN TRAGEDY

*The Waffle House shooting is a painful reminder of
Tennessee's failure to protect its own citizens
from mass murderers with guns.*

APRIL 23, 2018

There is something fundamentally democratic about a Waffle House restaurant in the wee hours of the morning. It's a place where people who have worked the late shift can stop for a hot meal on the way home, where high school kids can extend prom night an hour or two longer, where twentysomethings jazzed on live music can wind down after a night on the town. The coffee is always fresh, and the counter staff has heard it all but will usually listen again if you need an ear. It's a uniquely American place.

There's something tragically, fundamentally American, too, about an angry young white man with a firearm killing a bunch of strangers who have done him no harm. That's what happened early Sunday morning, when a man who was naked except for a green jacket loaded with ammunition opened fire with an AR-15 rifle at a Waffle House in the Antioch section of Nashville. Four people were fatally shot and four others were wounded before James Shaw Jr., an unarmed customer, wrestled the gun from him, saving untold lives.

The attacker ran away, shedding the jacket as he fled. Also left in his wake: Akilah DaSilva, DeEbony Groves, Joe Perez, and Taurean C. Sanderlin, all dead. All were in their twenties. All were people of color.

A search of the truck the gunman left behind led investigators to Travis Reinking, an Illinois man who had moved to Nashville only last fall. Considered armed and dangerous, Mr. Reinking immediately went to the top of the Tennessee Bureau of Investigation's most-wanted list. After some thirty-four hours at large in a cold rain, he was apprehended Monday afternoon clothed and wearing a backpack containing a loaded semiautomatic handgun.

For months, Mr. Reinking had shown "signs of significant instability," according to Don Aaron, a spokesman for the Metropolitan Nashville Police Department. He believed that the musician Taylor Swift was stalking him, and he had been arrested by Secret Service agents last summer for crossing a security barrier at the White House, insisting that as "a sovereign citizen," he had a right to speak with the president. The Southern Poverty Law Center, which tracks hate groups, links the "sovereign citizen" movement to the belief that Black Americans have fewer rights than whites.

After the White House incident, an investigation by the FBI office in Springfield, Illinois, led the sheriff's office of Tazewell County to confiscate Mr. Reinking's guns, but deputies returned them to his father, a transfer that Illinois law permits. On Sunday, Mr. Aaron said the father "has now acknowledged giving them back to his son."

We don't need to press play on the gun lobby's soundtrack to predict the response from politicians and right-wing media to this tragedy. Thoughts and prayers. This is no time for politics. Thoughts and prayers. We don't have a gun problem; we have a mental illness problem. Thoughts and prayers. Parents today can't control their kids. More thoughts and more prayers, none of which have done anything to stop the violence. You would think the entire Republican Party would be mired in a collective crisis of faith by now.

Blame Mr. Reinking's father, who clearly made a calamitous decision to trust his own troubled child, for the tragedy. Blame the stigma of mental illness, which may have made it feel impossible for the young man to seek help. Blame racist websites that fan hatred against people of color. Blame them all. The truth is, we know very little about what motivated Mr. Reinking, who is refusing to talk to the police.

But while we're spreading blame, let's not forget to save a generous portion for members of the Tennessee General Assembly, who are so busy passing legislation designed to punish the state's left-leaning cities that they have passed no legislation to protect their own citizens from maniacs with guns.

Actually, let's be very clear: they've done worse than nothing. Instead, they've expanded gun rights to such an extreme that Tennessee is now the go-to place for gun transfers that wouldn't be permissible in other places. This month, *The Knoxville News Sentinel* reported that the FBI had identified Tennessee as a "source state" in a pipeline that transferred guns and ammunition from unwitting private sellers in Tennessee to black market buyers in California, including at least one convicted felon. "It is very common for suppliers of firearms to obtain their supply from states with more lenient firearms laws, which are also known as source states," Kimberly Vesling, an FBI agent, explained.

Tennessee has some of the most permissive gun laws in the country, though no one seems to know whether Tennessee law prohibits a man whose right to own a gun has been revoked by another state from owning the same gun in Tennessee. The weapons "would not have been lawfully in his hands in Illinois," Nashville's police chief, Steve

Anderson, said of Mr. Reinking at a news conference on Sunday. "Now, possessing them in Tennessee, I don't know that he would have violated any Tennessee law."

Here's what we do know: because Republicans in the Tennessee General Assembly—owned lock, stock, and soul by the National Rifle Association—will not require people here to register their guns, four beautiful human beings with their whole lives ahead of them are being mourned by an entire city, and all the thoughts and prayers in the world will not bring them back to us.

THE PASSION OF SOUTHERN CHRISTIANS

*The president my fellow believers elected is about to
show them what betrayal really looks like.*

APRIL 8, 2017

In the world of apostolic betrayals, it's Judas who gets the headlines, but the everyday believer is more apt to fall in line behind Peter. Coldly handing Jesus over to his death in exchange for thirty pieces of silver was an over-the-top, cartoon-level move, but Peter's terrified denial of the man he believed to be the savior of the world? That one seems immensely human to me.

I have a lot of sympathy for Peter these days. Here it is, nearly Easter, and for the first time in my life I don't want anyone to know I'm a believer. To many, "Christian" has become synonymous with angry white voters in red hats, personally responsible for handcuffing all those undocumented mothers and wrenching them out of their sobbing children's arms.

Southern Christians tend to vote Republican, but in truth the values of the rural South are not incompatible with the policies of the Democratic Party. Our famed Southern hospitality is just an illustration of Jesus's exhortation to welcome the stranger. And consider what happens here whenever there's a flood or a tornado: long before the government agencies mobilize, local churches are taking up donations, cooking hot meals, helping people pick through the wreckage—helping everyone, no matter their religion or the color of their skin or the language they speak at home.

But as with a lot of people, including secular liberals, the way Christians behave as human beings can be deeply at odds with the way they vote. Decades ago, when I was still a teenager in Alabama, I heard my grandmother refer to some new neighbors as the Tallyho Boys. Turns out a gay couple had moved to a farm just down the road from her. The ladies of that rural community welcomed the couple with pound cakes and homemade jelly, but would they have voted for a political candidate who supported marriage equality? Not a chance.

Partly this divide comes down to scale: you can love a human being and still fear the group that person belongs to. A friend of mine recently joined a continuing-ed class made up about equally of native-born Americans and immigrants. The two groups integrate seamlessly, joking around like any coworkers, but the day after the election my friend said, "I think half my class might've just voted to deport the other half."

Tribal bonds have always been a challenge for our species. What's new is how baldly the 2016 election exposed the collision between basic Christian values and Republican Party loyalty. By any conceivable definition, the sitting president of the United States is the utter antithesis of Christian values—a misogynist who disdains refugees, persecutes immigrants, condones torture, and is energetically working to dismantle the safety net that protects our most vulnerable neighbors. Watching Christians put him in the White House has completely broken my heart.

My husband and I are cradle Catholics, but my husband's late aunt used to refer to us as "cafeteria Catholics," picking and choosing what we believe. Belonging to a community,

feeling at home in the liturgy, carrying on a long family tradition—all these intangibles made it easy enough, before the
election, to ignore much of what the church gets wrong and
to concentrate on what it gets right: supporting immigration,
welcoming refugees, opposing capital punishment, housing
the homeless, feeding the hungry, caring for the sick and the
aged and the lonely. Jesus said, "Truly I tell you, whatever
you did for one of the least of these brothers and sisters of
mine, you did for me." All the rest is window dressing.

But this is the part of Christ's message that most conservative Christians ignore when they step into the voting
booth. In part that's because abortion has become the ultimate
border wall for Southern believers. I can't count the number
of Christians I know who are one-plank voters: they'd put
Vladimir Putin in the White House if he promised to overturn
Roe v. Wade. To someone who ardently believes abortion is
murder, that idea is not as crazy as it seems. But people can
disagree on the moment when human life begins, and I don't
see my own commitment to protecting a woman's legal right
to choose as a contradiction of my religious practice. No
matter how you define it, protecting human life should never
stop at the zygote.

Republicans now have what they've long wanted: the
chance to turn this into a Christian nation. But what's being
planned in Washington will hit my fellow Southerners harder
than almost anyone else. Where are the immigrants? Mostly
in the South. Which states execute more prisoners? The
Southern states. Which region has the highest poverty rate?
The South. Where are you most likely to drink poisoned
water? Right here in the South. Where is affordable health
care hardest to find? You guessed it. My people are among
the least prepared to survive a Trump presidency, but the

"Christian" president they elected is about to demonstrate exactly what betrayal really looks like.

Liberal Christians in the South are by definition a lonely bunch, different from conservative Christians at home and different from secular liberals everywhere else. Still, I have never felt lonelier than I feel in Donald Trump's America.

But I also believe in resurrection. Every day brings word of a new Trump-inflicted human rights calamity, and every day a resistance is growing that I would not have imagined possible, a coalition of people on the left and the right who have never before seen themselves as allies. In working together, I hope we'll end up with a better nation, caring for the least among us and loving our neighbors as ourselves.

CHRISTIANS NEED A NEW
RIGHT-TO-LIFE MOVEMENT

*I hope for the time when feeding the hungry, caring for
the sick, and welcoming refugees aren't political issues.*

DECEMBER 24, 2017

At least since Martin Luther nailed his theses to the church door in 1517, Christians have disagreed on what Jesus calls them to do in the name of faith. There are nearly thirty-four thousand Christian denominations worldwide, a number that doesn't account for American Christians—nearly one in six, according to a Gallup poll last summer—who belong to no denomination.

But as lively as Christian debate can be, the special Senate election in Alabama has exposed how closely conservative Christianity is now in lockstep with the Republican Party. I grew up in Alabama, and I don't doubt the sincerity of my fellow believers on the other side of the political aisle, but when faithful Christians vote for a man credibly accused of child molesting, something is terribly wrong with Christianity. (With white Christianity, that is: Black Christians overwhelmingly supported the Democratic candidate, Doug Jones.) Eighty percent of those who voted for the Republican, Roy Moore, were white born-again Christians, and there is no skirting the damage they've done to their own moral standing.

The day of the election, the editor in chief of *Christianity Today*, Mark Galli, identified the biggest loser in Alabama:

Christian faith itself. From now on, Mr. Galli wrote, "When it comes to either matters of life and death or personal commitments of the human heart, no one will believe a word we say, perhaps for a generation."

Christianity presents a conundrum for evangelicals considering a monstrous political candidate who is also a Christian. The very foundation of our faith lies in the infinite mercy of a loving God, and it's hard for an ordinary sinner to cast the first stone. Last year I asked an evangelical friend how she could bring herself to support a presidential candidate like Donald Trump, whose behavior is so at odds with her own. "He says he's changed," she said, "and I believe in God's redemption. If I didn't, how could I get out of bed in the morning?"

I believe in redemption myself, though if I were in charge of things I think I'd be looking for evidence of repentance, too. And I'd be asking why people so deeply invested in redemption also tend to be so deeply invested in sending their fellow human beings to death row. But I'm trying to understand the country I've found myself in since last year's election, and these days I look hard for common ground.

It isn't easy to find. In her new book *Moral Combat: How Sex Divided American Christians and Fractured American Politics*, R. Marie Griffith explains the divide between liberal and conservative Christians as a casualty of "the sex wars"— disagreements over women's rights, birth control, abortion, and LGBTQ issues. By the time the Supreme Court's *Obergefell v. Hodges* decision legalized same-sex marriage in 2015, she writes, "the rupture between Christian antagonists in the sex wars felt irremediable: one could plausibly argue that American Christianity had flat out split into two virtually nonoverlapping religions."

What Christians need is a new right-to-life movement, one in which we agree to disagree about contentious issues of sexuality and focus instead on what we share, on what we all believe. Jesus had nothing to say about birth control or abortion or homosexuality. He did have quite a lot to say about the poor and the vulnerable, and maybe that's a good place to start.

Surely Christians across the political spectrum believe we're called to feed the hungry, heal the sick, protect the weak, and welcome the stranger. If we can agree on that much, and if we can keep our shrieking differences from wrecking the quiet conviction of shared belief, we could create a culture of life that has a chance of transcending the sex wars. I find myself hoping for a day when conservative Christian voters can elect conservative representatives for whom feeding the hungry and caring for the sick and welcoming refugees aren't political issues.

Here in Nashville, through an ecumenical program called Room in the Inn, nearly two hundred congregations of many faiths take in our homeless neighbors during the winter months. Every night from November through March, volunteers arrive downtown at the program's base of operations to pick up around 250 homeless people and drive them to area churches. Guests get a good meal, a hot shower, and a clean bed for the night. The next morning they get breakfast and a sack lunch to take when another set of volunteers arrives to drive them back downtown. That night the cycle starts all over again with different congregations.

The other day, I found a toddler's sippy cup lodged between the seats in the third row of my minivan. Our youngest child is nineteen, and we have no grandchildren. I held it, puzzled, until finally it dawned on me: my husband had taken his shift at Room in the Inn the night before, and this cup must belong to one of the families he drove to our church.

Babies without homes. The very thought is enough to make a person weep.

It's Christmas, the day Christians celebrate a baby wrapped in swaddling clothes and lying in a manger because there was no room for his family at the inn. We owe it to that infant to do better by the babies here among us. To do better by their parents, trying so hard to keep them fed and clothed and healthy. We owe it to him to throw open our arms and the doors of our inns. "You who are hungry and hurting and alone and afraid, come inside," we will say. "You belong here."

SHAME AND SALVATION IN
THE AMERICAN SOUTH

*I'm tempted to say I've never lived through a worse time
to be a sentient human being below the Mason-Dixon
line, but I know that's not true.*

MAY 20, 2019

The news emanating from the American South this year has been one long litany of assaults against human decency. In Alabama, a physician who performs an abortion in the case of rape may soon spend more time in prison than the rapist himself. In Mississippi, a family is suing their county and its sheriff for beating a Black man to death in jail. Tennessee just executed a deeply repentant Christian convert who had lived an exemplary life in prison. Proponents of a "culture of life" don't seem to recognize the incoherence of their position.

Unsurprisingly, the news about race relations is no better. Four fraternity members at the University of Georgia were expelled when an overtly racist video came to light. Fires at three historically Black churches in one Louisiana parish are being investigated as cases of arson. A South Carolina man was sentenced to ten years in prison for attempting to hire a white supremacist to lynch his Black neighbor. And don't even get me started on all the new voter-suppression tactics. White Southerners in power have been trying to keep Black people from voting ever since they got the right to vote.

I'm tempted to say that I've never lived through a worse time to be a sentient human being in the American South, but I know that's not true. I spent my entire 1960s childhood in Alabama, and I don't care how bad you think it is right now, it's nothing to the days when Bull Connor and his ilk still walked the earth. But it's also true that things can be "better" and still be shamefully, irredeemably bad.

Nevertheless, I find myself bristling as stereotypes of "redneck" Southerners fly around every time news of some fresh racist or misogynistic travesty hits social media. Here's a typical tweet (with expletives removed): "It's really easy to #BoycottAlabama because who the [expletive] would ever want to go to that redneck [expletive] on purpose?" As if every person in the entire state can be painted with the same brush. As if the presence of something indisputably evil obviates every good thing that happens within state borders. As if such statements aren't a transparent form of prejudice itself.

It's not that I don't understand the anger. The fury of a blue-state outsider can't possibly *touch* the fury of someone like me—someone who lives in one of these states, someone who is actually subject to these dangerous laws.

But even in these dark days, when vicious people stand brazenly on street corners holding hateful signs, anger is not the only thing I feel. Living here, I also know how much of this life defies flyover-country prejudice. I know that Southern hospitality is a real thing, and that it isn't race contingent. I know that the transcendent natural beauty of this region matches the majesty of any other place on earth. I know how very many people here are fighting to make life safer and more equitable for everyone, even for those who keep voting to make life less safe and less fair for everyone else.

These heroes aren't lobbing insults on Twitter. They are working for actual change. I'm talking about Springboard to Opportunities in Jackson, Mississippi. About Tennesseans for Alternatives to the Death Penalty and Conexión Américas and the Nashville Food Project and the Tennessee Justice Center here in Nashville. About the Georgia Justice Project and the Southern Center for Human Rights in Atlanta. About the Equal Justice Initiative in Montgomery, Alabama. (Yes, Alabama.) About the Center for Ethical Living and Social Justice Renewal in New Orleans and the Conservation Voters of South Carolina. About the Southern Environmental Law Center in offices all across the South.

That's only a minor portion, the tiniest portion, of a gargantuan list of social justice organizations around the South that would stagger the imagination of any anti-Southern ranter on Twitter.

But even more than these vital and necessary organizations, it's the regular people who give me hope. The worried Southerners who didn't leave. The worried Southerners who vote for change (and volunteer on Election Day to help others vote for change), who write their elected representatives time and time and time again, who support the full-time advocates with funding and social media shares and everything else they can think of. The worried Southerners who work to preserve what's good about this beleaguered region and to heal what's hateful.

I was thinking about all this last month when I went to a fundraiser for the Vanderbilt University Libraries at the historic Belcourt Theatre here in Nashville. The headliners were a group of writers who embody everything I love most about the South. In 1998, songwriters Matraca Berg and Marshall Chapman worked with novelists Jill McCorkle and Lee Smith to create a musical they called *Good Ol' Girls*. (*The Times* called it "a feminist-literary country music revue.") Ever since then, the writers have gotten together once a year or so, always as a benefit for a worthy cause, to perform stories and songs that collectively capture this region and its people. The stories they tell and the songs they sing are hilarious and sad, both at once—wholly, observably, intricately human. They explain what it feels like to be female and Southern and, most often, struggling in one way or another.

Here in the South, it's the struggle that so often defines us. We're struggling here, and sometimes people who struggle latch on to false promises and fall for lies peddled by snake-oil salesmen masquerading as leaders. Sometimes the struggle makes us mean, and sometimes it makes us stingy, and it almost always breaks our hearts.

But the struggle is also what makes us tell funny stories and write gorgeous songs. It's also what makes us get up and fight back. I won't even try to argue that what you see coming out of statehouses and frat houses down here isn't the true South. It is. But it isn't the *only* true South. Please believe me when I tell you this: we are fighting back.

TEXAS ISN'T THE PROBLEM

Disasters call for compassion, not sniping
on social media.

FEBRUARY 22, 2021

Last week's fierce winter storms didn't change all that much at our house. We got mostly snow and sleet here, not freezing rain, so we never lost power. The roads were a catastrophic mess, but our refrigerator and cupboards were full—it's a time-honored Southern tradition to clear store shelves of milk and bread when the forecast calls for even a flake of snow—and we didn't have to risk our lives to get to work because we can do our work from home. We were lucky.

That's all in the world it was: pure dumb luck.

Others were not nearly so fortunate. More than four million people lost power in Texas. Hundreds of thousands of other Americans—mainly in the South, where such weather has historically been an anomaly—soon found themselves in the same boat. Pipes froze. Roadways were lethal. Makeshift attempts to keep warm turned deadly. Vaccine distribution came to a halt.

Weather-related disasters used to be called acts of God: events that are rare, unforeseen, and above all nobody's fault. You don't blame people living in trailers for the tornado that turned their homes into twisted wreckage. You don't blame drowning people for the flooded river. An act of God might engender a crisis of faith, but in the old days it didn't cause a crisis of community. If you were untouched

94

by disaster, you felt lucky, and you rolled up your sleeves to help the ones who weren't.

You certainly didn't tell suffering people *in the midst of a deadly crisis* that they had brought their suffering on themselves.

"Hey, Texas!" the novelist Stephen King wrote in a tweet that has been liked or shared by nearly one hundred thousand people. "Keep voting for officials who don't believe in climate change and supported privatization of the power grid!" He failed to mention the three hundred thousand citizens of hyper-liberal Portland, Oregon, who also lost power in the storm.

Liberals, of course, weren't the only ones playing the blame game in the media last week. In Texas, electricity comes primarily from fossil fuels, but that didn't stop Texas governor Greg Abbott from peddling the lie that power outages in Texas were the fault of, get this, renewable energy. Never mind that the frozen wind turbines in his state represent only a small fraction of the energy lost to failures in natural gas production during the freeze. Or that there are ways to keep turbines from freezing in the first place.

This whole conversation was playing out while people were freezing to death in their homes and dying of carbon monoxide poisoning in their cars. While people were burning their belongings to keep warm and frantically trying to find backup power for oxygen-dependent family members. And none of it had anything to do with their voting record.

It's important to note that not all Southerners believe the lies about climate change trotted out by Republican politicians enslaved to the fossil fuel industry. Southern Republicans tell their constituents many, many lies, and plenty of people believe them. But not all of us. Nowhere near all of us. In the 2020 presidential election, 5,259,126 Texans voted for Joe Biden. That's more than 46 percent of voters in the state, and it's a fairly safe bet that those folks believe in climate change.

But does it even matter? Does how someone votes determine their worth as a human being? It doesn't take a degree in ethics to understand that people don't deserve to die just because they made the mistake of trusting greedy, power-mad liars to tell them the truth.

Predictably, the Texas politicians who deny the reality of climate change and the utility executives who mismanaged the Texas power grid weren't the ones who suffered the most in last week's winter storms. And the people who were hardest hit—residents of minority neighborhoods—sure couldn't jet off to Cancún with Ted Cruz to escape the cold. "Let them eat snow" indeed.

There will be investigations into the full array of reasons for the power failures, and Texas officials may even pull themselves together enough to make a plan for mitigating the damage from future extreme weather events. But at this point there is no stopping the weather calamities themselves.

We don't know for a fact that these particular storms were the result of an unstable climate, though there is science to support that theory. What we do know is that extreme weather is no longer remarkable. The hundred-year floods of old—like the hundred-year hurricanes and the hundred-year forest fires and the hundred-year winter storms—are happening far more often now, and their frequency will continue to rise.

These are not acts of God. These are acts of human behavior, the erratic weather patterns of a climate we have incinerated. And as they always do, the poor and the disenfranchised will suffer the most from the damage we've done.

In this context, the impulse to take a cheap shot at Southerners on Twitter isn't remotely as dangerous as the impulse to deny climate change itself, but it matters. Every form of prejudice matters, perhaps especially so when the people who keep pointing out the splinter in someone else's eye are trying to see around a plank in their own.

Where climate-related weather disasters are concerned, none of us is innocent. We all created this emergency. With our gasoline engines and our chemically fertilized crops and our factory farms and our addiction to plastic and paper towels, we're all guilty. And if we have so far escaped the worst ravages of that unstable climate, we need to admit that it's not because of how we vote or who we are or what we believe. It's just luck. Just pure dumb luck. And it's time to roll up our sleeves.

GOING TO CHURCH WITH
JIMMY CARTER

One cure for troubled faith: a Sunday school lesson
taught by the former president.

APRIL 16, 2018

I knew I was in trouble as soon as I pulled into the parking lot of the Quality Inn in Americus, Georgia, last Saturday night. It was long past dark, but I could see well enough to note the out-of-state license plates—New Mexico, Pennsylvania, California, Alaska—places far from this peanut-farming land.

We were all there for the same reason: to see Jimmy Carter teach Sunday school at the Maranatha Baptist Church in the nearby town of Plains. And if the crowded parking lot was any indication, finding a seat the next morning would be a challenge.

After the inauguration of Ronald Reagan in 1981, President Carter returned to Plains, his hometown. Throughout the longest and most influential post-presidency in American history, he has continued teaching Sunday school, and the public is always welcome to sit in.

President Carter's commitment to human rights—executed largely though Habitat for Humanity and the Carter Center, which works to eradicate poverty and disease and cultivate democracy—earned him a Nobel Peace Prize in 2002. In his acceptance address, Carter said, "God gives us the capacity for choice. We can choose to alleviate suffering.

We can choose to work together for peace." Even when he isn't teaching Sunday school, his unwavering Christian faith informs everything he says and does.

My own faith in religious and democratic institutions has not been so unwavering, especially not since white Christians put a demagogue in the White House. But I have always wanted to go to his Sunday school class. When President Carter, now ninety-three, announced that he was cutting back on his teaching schedule at the church and publishing a new book—*Faith: A Journey for All*—it seemed almost like a sign. Jimmy Carter still has faith in this country, and I hoped his Sunday school lesson might restore my faith, too.

The sanctuary of the Maranatha Baptist Church seats 350 people, and there's a spillover room with a live video feed for another 100 or so. "Based on recent attendance trends, visitors who arrived before 6 a.m. had no problem obtaining a sanctuary seat," the church's website reads.

In my motel room I set the alarm for an hour I haven't seen since 1998, the last time there was a newborn baby in my house. Fifteen minutes before it went off, I heard the pipes rattling as someone in the next room took a shower, so I jumped in the shower myself. Trying to beat a total stranger to Sunday school is not exactly in the spirit of Christian charity, but I wanted a seat in that sanctuary.

In springtime, rural southwest Georgia is as pretty a place as you will find on this earth—wildflowers swathing the fallow fields and blooming along the edges of red soil already plowed for planting, bluebirds hunting from fence posts, mockingbirds sending dueling songs into the pines— but I couldn't see any of that from Highway 280 in the pre-dawn darkness.

99

I arrived at the church and was given a number—forty-one—and told to park in the pecan orchard because the lot was already full. At 7:45 it would be time to get in line to be checked by the Secret Service. I wasn't there early enough to be guaranteed a seat in the sanctuary, a church member said, but it wasn't out of the realm of possibility.

Thanks to the early riser in the motel room next door, I made it into the sanctuary. While we waited for President Carter to arrive, I chatted with a Baptist minister sitting in the pew behind me about a recent interview with Stephen Colbert, in which Mr. Carter hinted that he considers the sitting president of the United States a liar. Asked what it takes to be president, he told Mr. Colbert, "I used to think it was to tell the truth. But I've changed my mind lately."

There were flashes of the same impish wit on display at the church in Plains. "Do we have any visitors this morning?" he joked to the crowd. He asked where we were all from, and voices sang out from places like Cameroon, Israel, Uzbekistan.

When it was time for the lesson itself, President Carter stood smiling and spoke without referring to notes, moving to the lectern only to read from the scripture. The text was from the Acts of the Apostles, passages concerning the priorities of the early church. "They worshiped together. They had fellowship together. And a third thing: they took care of each other's needs, even in a sacrificial way," he said. He spoke particularly about the generosity of Barnabas, who sold his own field and gave the money to Jesus's apostles to distribute to the needy.

President Carter is not a pacing, gesturing, booming-voiced orator, but he is a brilliant teacher—moving nimbly between his memories, his concerns for the world, and what the Acts have to say about the right relationship of human beings to one another. He asks questions, nods encouragement when an answer is close but keeps nudging until someone hits on the point he's trying to make.

"We have lost faith in a lot of things that have always nurtured us," he said. "Many people in the world have lost faith in democracy. We've lost faith in the sanctity of telling the truth and the value of education. We've lost faith in the equality of people. In our country's history, some of our greatest struggles have been over the issue of equality."

Then he asked the congregation what year women in the United States gained the right to vote.

Several called out "1920!" But it was a trick question. In the Jim Crow South, at least, "that was white women," he reminded us. "A lot of white people don't remember that distinction."

He spoke movingly about his first security briefing as president-elect, about the solemn responsibility of the country's commander in chief to safeguard nuclear weapons. "If we don't figure out as collective human beings how to get along with each other, even the people we don't like and with whom we don't agree—say the Americans and the Russians, the Americans and the Chinese, the Americans and anybody else—if we don't figure out collectively how to get along with each other and take care of each other, that might be the end of humanity."

President Carter is a realist, and he's concerned about the current state of the world, but he was also careful to say he doesn't believe the worst will happen—"I'm a Christian, and I believe God's will and God's love will prevail, but I worry about it." And he returned again to his call to "take care of each other, even the people that we don't like, even our enemies." At the Maranatha Baptist Church, a Sunday school lesson is a master class in responsibility and goodness and, above all, love.

He reminded the congregation that Barnabas was known among the early Christians as "the encourager." And encouragement is clearly something Jimmy Carter knows a great deal about.

SOCIAL
JUSTICE

WHAT IS AMERICA TO ME?

*I found the heart of my own country
in a classroom full of newcomers.*

JULY 22, 2017

In 2015, just as refugees were pouring out of Syria and pictures of terrified children filled every newscast and front page in the world, a notice appeared in my church bulletin: "Are you looking for a way to help our city's newest refugees?" It was a call for volunteers to assist in an English-language classroom at a local public school. I was once a high school literature teacher, so I saved the bulletin, planning to follow through whenever life slowed down a little. More than a year later, I was still dithering. The day after Donald Trump was elected, I finally volunteered.

The sun was just rising when I left for my first class. I'd been away from school for twenty years, and I was a little nervous, but when I walked through those doors I felt instantly at home. In the school office three mirrors hang side by side, each marked by the kind of inspirational message schools specialize in: "College Ready." "Career Ready." "Life Ready." While I signed the visitors' log, two students wearing hijabs hugged each other goodbye in the bright corridor, and the principal switched on the intercom to lead the Pledge of Allegiance.

Teachers at this school face all the challenges of any teacher in a building full of teenagers, but in the Trump era their job is incalculably harder. My oldest son is a middle

school teacher at another Nashville school with a large immigrant population. On November 9, his students arrived in
class shaken, aware of what the new administration would
mean for their families. Already a man had thrown a can
from his car window at the older sister of one student, yelling
"Terrorist!" as he passed.

"Build that wall! Build that wall!" The chants at Trump
rallies are chilling, vicious, the voice of a mob, but among the
many conservatives I know—those who voted for Mr. Trump
and those who didn't—there is not a single person who would
throw a can at a child or assume that a Middle Eastern–born
teenager must be a terrorist. They welcome immigrants who
are here legally, but they argue for a level playing field, where
newcomers are bound by the same rules they are bound by
themselves. So Tennessee's official attitude toward immigrants is what you'd expect from the conservative South: it
joined fifteen other states in signing an amicus brief supporting President Trump's travel ban.

Nashville has one of the fastest-growing immigrant
populations in the country. Close to 12 percent of the city's
residents are foreign-born, and 30 percent of public school
students speak a language other than English at home.

The city has made a point of welcoming international
newcomers, despite the actions of the Tennessee General
Assembly, which meets in the heart of downtown. Metro
schools don't inquire about immigration status; instead, they
offer mentors to foreign-born families. Workers at the city's
public libraries help newcomers apply for citizenship. Metro
police officers don't check the immigration status of people
pulled over for traffic violations. The uneasiness here is pal-
pable even so. Seventy percent of Nashville residents support
a path to citizenship for undocumented immigrants, but

such numbers offer little reassurance when Immigration and Customs Enforcement agents posed as Metro police officers during a recent roundup of Nashville Kurds.

The challenge of teaching "English learners," as they are called in Metro schools, is immense, and this political climate only adds to the complexity of the task. The students in an English-learners classroom speak many different languages at home, and their English-language competence varies widely. Every single step in the process of speaking—or listening, or reading, or writing—must be broken down and explained. To borrow a line from Joan Didion, English is a language I play by ear, and volunteering in this classroom has taught me more about my native tongue than graduate school did.

A typical class includes a lesson followed by a chance to work in pairs, taking turns reading (or speaking) and listening (or writing). As the students work, the teacher moves from table to table, and my job is to do the same, answering questions or serving as a partner for a student without one. At times I'm flummoxed by a student's question, and then all the other kids at the table pitch in to explain. They don't speak one another's languages, either, but they understand better than I do what's puzzling about the lesson, and they help one another—and sometimes me—understand.

Talking with these teenagers, I'm always struck by how familiar they seem. There's the class clown, raising his hand to ask a silly question that makes his classmates laugh. There's the school beauty, who never leaves her seat—she knows the others, vying to be her partner, will come to her if she waits. There's the sleepy kid trying to nap undetected behind an open book, and the type A kid with a hand always in the air. Their clothes and hairstyles are different, but they seem exactly like the suburban students I once taught;

exactly like my own three sons, the youngest still a teenager himself; exactly like my high school classmates.

Only they aren't exactly alike. Because they live in a nation with an incoherent and punitive immigration policy, these students—new residents of a growing, multicultural city—are as vulnerable as any immigrants in the red-state countryside. They live with the inescapable fear of deportation, their own or a loved one's, and yet they come to class every day to master the language and culture of their difficult new home. In this effort, teachers are their staunchest allies.

In the English-learners classroom, there's more to learn than language. During a unit on the Harlem Renaissance, I arrived to find a bulletin board fashioned from an assignment modeled on Countee Cullen's "Heritage." The poem begins, "What is Africa to me?"

The students' own poems were titled "What Is Myanmar to Me?" ("Spicy foods, we'll take seconds, please") and "What Is Zambia to Me?" ("I can feel the hot weather in my body / A beautiful sun outside on my face") and "What Is Mexico to Me?" ("I'm like a flame, / Waiting for go back again")—on and on and on. I stood before that bulletin board with my back turned to hide my tears, and I read every poem.

School's out for summer now, but I can't stop thinking about all those brand-new Americans recalling the countries of their birth, using poetry to convey the beauty of home. English is a problematic language, but these students are working hard to learn it—and working harder still to belong.

ICE CAME TO TAKE THEIR NEIGHBOR. THEY SAID NO.

It is the story of David and Goliath,
of Hansel and Gretel, of Robin Hood.

AUGUST 5, 2019

Residents of a quiet working-class neighborhood in the Hermitage section of Nashville woke up very early on July 22 to find officials from Immigration and Customs Enforcement trying to arrest one of their own.

An unmarked pickup truck with flashing red and blue lights had pulled into the man's driveway, blocking his van. Two ICE agents armed with an administrative warrant ordered the man and his twelve-year-old son to step out of their vehicle. The man, who had lived in the neighborhood for some fourteen years, did exactly what the Tennessee Immigrant and Refugee Rights Coalition urges immigrants to do in such cases: he stayed put.

An administrative warrant gives officials permission to detain a suspect, but it does not allow them to enter his house or vehicle. The ICE officials in that Nashville driveway were apparently counting on the man not to know that. With an administrative warrant, "there's no judicial review, no magistrate review, no probable cause," Daniel Ayoade Yoon, a lawyer later summoned to the house by immigration activists, told the *Nashville Scene*. He told WTVF, "They were saying, 'If you don't come out, we're going to arrest you, we're going to arrest your twelve-year-old son.'" The administrative warrant they held did not give them the authority to do either.

Neighbors witnessing the standoff were appalled. "We was like, 'Oh my God, are you serious?'" Angela Glass told WPLN. "And that's when everybody got mad and was like, 'They don't do nothing, they don't bother nobody, you haven't got no complaints from them. Police have never been called over there. All they do is work and take care of their family and take care of the community.'"

Another neighbor, Stacey Farley, told WTVF, "The family don't bother nobody, they work every day, they come home, the kids jump on their trampoline. It's just a community."

More neighbors joined the scene and urged the man and his son not to listen to the agents. As temperatures rose in the hot Tennessee sun, they brought water and food and cool rags. They refilled the van's gas tank so the man could keep his air conditioner running. "We stuck together like neighbors are supposed to do," Felishadae Young told WZTV.

ICE officials summoned the Nashville police for backup. The officers who arrived stood nearby but did not intervene. State law prohibits any Tennessee community from designating itself a sanctuary city, but the police here don't get involved in civil immigration cases. "We're not here to enforce any federal script," Sergeant Noah Smith told *The Tennessean*. "We're just here if anything major happens."

More than four hours later, ICE agents finally abandoned their efforts and drove away, though everyone on the scene expected them to return. Neighbors and activists linked arms to form a human chain from the van to the door of the house. The man and his son dashed inside. A woman came to the door and in Spanish tearfully thanked bystanders for their help. Shortly thereafter, the family fled.

This story of one undocumented family in one hard-working neighborhood of one growing Southern city generated national attention, with articles appearing in outlets as disparate as *Essence*, *The Washington Post*, *The Miami Herald*, *The Cut*, *CBS News*, and *The New York Post*. There's a reason for the widespread interest.

Inconsequential as this story might appear to be when balanced against the great travesty of American immigration policy today, it nevertheless gives us hope. It is the story of David and Goliath, of Hansel and Gretel, of Robin Hood. It is the story of weakness defeating strength. It reminds us, in this cynical age, of what is still good in us, of what we are yet capable of, even against great odds.

From our earliest days, we feel the suffering of our own kind. A babe in arms, hearing another infant's wailing, will begin to cry for no reason other than shared distress. Instinctively we understand the truth of the Reverend Dr. Martin Luther King Jr.'s statement in his great "Letter from Birmingham Jail": "Injustice anywhere is a threat to justice everywhere."

So we salute the heroes of Hermitage—the ordinary people who, like the rest of us, are absorbed by their own worries, contending with their own troubles, but who nevertheless turned from their own lives to protect their neighbor, to shield him from the lies and tricks of the very government that was formed to protect his rights. We celebrate their courage in the face of unwarranted authority, and we take heart from their commitment to justice. We replay the video again and again to watch them link arms, to watch them calling out words of comfort and encouragement. We remember a truth that has lately been too easy to forget: we belong to one another.

CHRISTMAS ISN'T COMING TO DEATH ROW

When it comes to the death penalty, guilt or innocence shouldn't really matter to Christians.

DECEMBER 10, 2018

Until August, Tennessee had not put a prisoner to death in nearly a decade. Last Thursday, it performed its third execution in four months.

This was not a surprising turn of events. In each case, recourse to the courts had been exhausted. In each case, Governor Bill Haslam, a Republican, declined to intervene, though there were many reasons to justify intervening. Billy Ray Irick suffered from psychotic episodes that raised profound doubts about his ability to distinguish right from wrong. Edmund Zagorksi's behavior in prison was so exemplary that even the warden pleaded for his life. David Earl Miller also suffered from mental illness and was a survivor of child abuse so horrific that he tried to kill himself when he was six years old.

Questions about the humanity of Tennessee's lethal-injection protocol were so pervasive following the execution of Mr. Irick that both Mr. Zagorski and Mr. Miller elected to die in Tennessee's electric chair, which was first used in 1916. (The state spruced it up in 1989.) Their choice says something very clear about Tennessee's three-drug execution cocktail, as Justice Sonia Sotomayor noted in a dissenting opinion to the Supreme Court's decision not to hear Mr.

Miller's case: "Both so chose even though electrocution can be a dreadful way to die," she wrote. "They did so against the backdrop of credible scientific evidence that lethal injection as currently practiced in Tennessee may well be even worse." Electrocution might not be any more humane than death by lethal injection, in other words, but at least it offers a speedier hideous death.

Presumably this is the same thinking behind the position taken by fifty-one death row prisoners in Alabama who want to die in an untested nitrogen gas chamber rather than by either the electric chair or lethal injection.

Nitrogen gas. That's where we are in the whole ungodly machinery of capital punishment: human beings are choosing to die by nitrogen gas.

Here in red-state America, the death penalty is supported by 73 percent of white evangelical Christians and by a solid majority of Catholics—53 percent, despite official church teaching to the contrary—according to a Pew Research Center survey released in June.

The three men Tennessee most recently executed were all convicted of especially brutal murders—in Mr. Irick's case, the rape and murder of a little girl left in his care; in Mr. Miller's, the murder of his girlfriend, a young woman with cognitive disabilities. Mr. Zagorksi murdered two men who were meeting him to buy a hundred pounds of marijuana with cash. Death row inmates are not sympathetic figures. Not that being sincerely remorseful and using your time in prison for genuine transformation gets you very far here in Execution Alley. In 1998, Texas executed a woman who became a born-again Christian while in prison. In 2015, Georgia executed a woman who had earned a theology degree on death row.

It's hard not to notice that all these inmates, rehabilitated or not, were killed in the Bible Belt, in states where a sizable portion of the population believes they live—or at least believes they should live—in a Christian nation. Mr. Miller was the second inmate in the South to be executed last week, and two more—one in Texas and one in Florida—will die at state hands by Thursday. That's a lot of killing for the thou-shalt-not-kill states and at a time of year that's particularly ironic. What is Advent, after all, but a time of waiting for the birth of a baby who will grow up to be executed himself?

For many anti-abortion Christians, there's no contradiction between taking a "pro-life" position against allowing a woman to choose whether to continue a pregnancy and taking a "tough on crime" position whose centerpiece is capital punishment. An unborn fetus, they argue, is innocent, while a prisoner on death row is by definition guilty.

But for a true "pro-life" Christian, guilt or innocence really shouldn't be the point. Cute and cuddly or brutish and unrepentant, human life is human life. It doesn't matter whether you like the human life involved. If you truly believe that human life is sacred, right down to an invisible diploid cell, then you have no business letting the state put people to death in your name, even if those people have committed hideous crimes.

There are numerous pragmatic reasons to abolish the death penalty. It doesn't deter crime. It doesn't save the state money. It risks ending an innocent life. (The Death Penalty Information Center lists the names of 164 innocent people who have been exonerated after serving years on death row. The most recent, Clemente Javier Aguirre-Jarquin, was released from a Florida prison just last month.) It is applied in a haphazard and irrational manner that disproportionately targets people of color. It puts prison staff in the position of executing a human being they know personally and often truly care for. But the real problem with the death penalty can't be summed up by setting pros and cons on different sides of a balance to see which carries more weight. The real problem of the death penalty is its human face.

A person on death row is a person. No matter how ungrieved he may be once he is gone, he is still a human being. And it is not our right to take his life any more than it was his right to take another's.

AN ACT OF MERCY IN TENNESSEE

*She was sixteen when she killed a man who paid to
have sex with her. In granting her clemency, Tennessee's
governor showed compassion, and political courage.*

JANUARY 14, 2019

In 2004, Johnny Allen, a real estate broker in his forties,
picked up a sixteen-year-old girl named Cyntoia Brown at
a drive-in restaurant here. Mr. Allen bought her some food
and then took her to his house, agreeing to pay her $150 for
sex. Ms. Brown shot him to death as he slept, taking his money
and two of his handguns with her when she fled in his truck.

It's easy to understand why prosecutors at Cyntoia
Brown's trial in 2006 saw this as a slam dunk case. A prostitute, a robbery, the cold-blooded murder of a sleeping man:
How much nuance can there be in such a scenario? The jury
apparently agreed, finding Ms. Brown guilty of first-degree
murder and aggravated robbery. She was sentenced to life
in prison. In 2012, the United States Supreme Court ruled
against sentencing juveniles to life without parole, but last
month the Tennessee Supreme Court upheld Ms. Brown's
sentence on the grounds that she would be eligible for parole
when she is sixty-nine years old.

But in the case of teenage criminals, even teenagers
guilty of the most hideous crimes, there are no slam dunk
cases. Ms. Brown's attorneys argued that she had killed Mr.
Allen in self-defense, fearing for her life, and that she had

taken his guns and his money out of fear of her pimp. (A 2011 documentary, *Me Facing Life: Cyntoia's Story*, details her enslavement to the pimp, who was known as Cut Throat.)

"If you look at Cyntoia's original transcripts, they are peppered with the phrase 'teen prostitute,'" Derri Smith, founder and chief executive of the nonprofit End Slavery Tennessee, told CNN. "We know today there's no such thing as a teen prostitute . . . because this teen may think that she decided this was her idea to be raped multiple times a day and give money to someone else, it's pretty clear there's an adult behind that who's manipulating and exploiting her."

On January 7, Governor Bill Haslam, a Republican, commuted Ms. Brown's sentence. She will be paroled on August 7, exactly fifteen years from the date of her arrest. "Cyntoia Brown committed, by her own admission, a horrific crime at the age of 16," Mr. Haslam said. "Yet, imposing a life sentence on a juvenile that would require her to serve at least 51 years before even being eligible for parole consideration is too harsh, especially in light of the extraordinary steps Ms. Brown has taken to rebuild her life. Transformation should be accompanied by hope."

It was an unexpected move. Harsh sentences aren't exactly rare in the red states, and Republican governors, even relatively moderate ones like Mr. Haslam, are generally loath to intervene. Last September, Mr. Haslam declined to commute the sentence of Edmund Zagorski, a death row prisoner who, like Ms. Brown, had lived an exemplary life in prison. In Mr. Zagorski's case, transformation was accompanied by execution.

There are differences here, of course: at the time of the murders, Ms. Brown was a minor being kept as a sex slave, while Mr. Zagorski was an adult dealing drugs. Politically, though, there are risks in showing compassion to any murderer. Mr. Haslam will soon be leaving office after eight years, it's true, but he is also the heir apparent to the United States Senate seat that will be vacated by Lamar Alexander in 2020.

In commuting Ms. Brown's sentence, Mr. Haslam was bucking a huge law-and-order contingent in this state. The six-member parole board that presided over Ms. Brown's clemency hearing last May was divided, with two recommending that her sentence be commuted to time served, two recommending parole after twenty-five years, and two recommending no clemency at all. The police detective who investigated the murder urged Mr. Haslam not to pardon her. "First and foremost, Cyntoia Brown did not commit this murder because she was a child sex slave as her advocates would like you to believe," he wrote in a letter to the governor. "Cyntoia Brown's motive for murdering Johnny Allen in his sleep was robbery."

It doesn't help Mr. Haslam's prospects that most of the voices calling for him to pardon Cyntoia Brown are political liabilities. Like Memphis, Nashville is a blue dot in the red sea of Tennessee, and the state legislature's highest priority seems to be passing laws that undercut liberal policies enacted by its two largest cities. So when the Metropolitan Council in Nashville unanimously voted to urge the governor to pardon Cyntoia Brown, and when Nashville's mayor, David Briley, later praised the governor's decision to offer clemency, they weren't doing Mr. Haslam any favors. Neither were celebrities like Ashley Judd, Rihanna, Amy Schumer, and Kim Kardashian West, all of whom have taken up Ms. Brown's cause over the years, or Representative Alexandria Ocasio-Cortez, a newly elected Democrat from New York, who tweeted her praise of Mr. Haslam.

He commuted Ms. Brown's sentence anyway.

It was an "act of mercy," according to Ms. Brown, and she thanked the governor in a statement: "I will do everything I can to justify your faith in me."

In this country we like to profess outrage at the primitive understanding of justice at work in other parts of the world—at the hangings, at the beheadings, at the murder sentences for extramarital affairs. But we live in a country where children can stand trial as adults and where our immigration policy includes separating nursing infants from their mothers pleading for asylum. Not everyone in other parts of the world adheres to such harsh notions of justice, and not everyone here adheres to the harsh border-control measures our president celebrates. There will always be disputes about what "justice" means.

As a country, we continue to get many questions of right and wrong entirely wrong. We seem to be a long way from knowing the difference between a crime motivated by evil and a crime motivated by profound fear, or desperation, or mental illness, or cognitive disability. We're a long way from understanding that the death penalty is not a deterrent to crime. A long way from recognizing that racial bias pervades our criminal justice system so thoroughly that despair is more common in many of our communities than justice will ever be.

But there is hope when the governor of Tennessee chooses mercy and understanding over the strict letter of the law. There is hope when a young woman can walk out of prison into the light of freedom after fifteen years behind bars for a crime she committed as an endangered and exploited child. We may never agree on what real justice looks like, but we will always know mercy when we see it. And mercy will do.

AN OPEN LETTER TO
WHITE CHRISTIANS

*Our sins are grievous, but we are not
yet beyond redemption.*

JUNE 8, 2019

Since long before it was a country, our country has been in flames. When we arrived on our big ships and decimated this land's original peoples with our viruses and our guns, when we used our Christian faith as a justification for killing both "heretic" and "heathen," we founded this country in flames. And every month, every week, every day, for the last four hundred years, we have been setting new fires.

White Christians who came before us captured human beings and beat them and raped them and stole their babies from them and stole their parents from them and stole their husbands and their wives from them and locked them in chains and made them work in inhuman conditions. Our spiritual ancestors went to church and listened to their pastors argue that these human beings weren't even human. Our pastors don't tell us that anymore, but we are still setting fires.

Christians set a fire every time we allow our leaders to weaponize our fears against us. We set a fire every time our faith in good police officers prevents us from seeing the bad ones. Christian voters preserve a system that permits police violence, unjust prosecutions, and hellhole prisons filled with people who should have received the same addiction treatment we give our own troubled kids.

We set a fire every time we fail to scrutinize a police culture that allows an officer's own fear and hatred to justify the most casual brutality against another human being. It would be almost unbelievable to match an adjective like "casual" with a noun like "brutality," but we have seen the videos. Watch the faces of justice shove an old man aside and leave him bleeding on the ground. Watch them drive their vehicles into protesters protected by the United States Constitution. Watch them fire rubber bullets directly at journalists doing work that is also protected by the United States Constitution. In video after video, note their unconcern with people who are bleeding or screaming in pain.

Make yourself look. Study the air of perfect nonchalance on Derek Chauvin's face as he kneels on the neck of George Floyd. Register the blithe indifference in his posture, the way he puts his hand in his pocket as though he were just walking along the street on a sunny summer day. Nothing in his whole body suggests concern. He is not the least bit troubled by taking another human life.

We created Derek Chauvin.

Every single aspect of our criminal justice system is permeated by racism, but too many Christians continue to vote for "law and order" candidates anyway, failing to notice that more cops and more weapons and more prisons have done exactly nothing to make us safer. Failing to notice that they have instead endangered all Americans, but Black Americans most of all.

We should know better by now. There are so many resources to help us know better, yet too many Christians ignore the history books that document the terrible legacy of slavery. We ignore the novelists who tell us why the caged bird sings. We ignore the poets who teach us the cruel cost of a dream deferred. In our carefully preserved ignorance, we pile all their books up in a great pyre, and we set them on fire.

We set the fire when we heard a peaceful crowd singing, "We shall overcome someday," and understood that someday would never be today, that someday was at best still decades and decades away. We set the fire when we heard a peaceful crowd singing, "Lean on me when you're not strong," and believed it was time to call in the military. We set the fire when our "Christian" president cleared a peaceful crowd by spraying them with tear gas as though they were enemy combatants, marched to a nearby church for a photo op, and held up a Bible to imply that God is on his side.

We have to stop letting this president turn our faith into a travesty. Love is the only way to put out this fire, love and listening and the hard work of changing, but this "Christian" president doesn't want to put out the fire. Fire is his homeplace. Fire is his native land.

Perhaps it is ours, as well.

"Blessed are the merciful," Jesus taught us, but we built prison after prison. "If anyone strikes you on the right cheek, turn to him the other also," Jesus taught us, but we did not turn our cheek. We turned instead our billy club. We turned instead our pepper spray. We turned instead our rubber bullets and our tear gas and our riot gear. To George Floyd, and to so many others, we turned instead our knee.

There are positive models for what Christian faith in the public sphere can look like. Think of John Alexander, a Baptist philosophy teacher who published a journal designed to convert white evangelicals to the cause of civil rights.

Think of the Reverend Daniel J. Berrigan, a Jesuit priest who opposed the Vietnam War. Think of the Reverend Jennifer Butler, a Presbyterian minister who founded the activist group Faith in Public Life. Here in Nashville we have the Reverend Stacy Rector, the Presbyterian executive director of Tennesseans for Alternatives to the Death Penalty, and the Reverend Becca Stevens, an Episcopal priest and founder of a nonprofit that works to "rise up against systems that commoditize, criminalize, and abuse women," as the Thistle Farms website puts it. There are many, many others, all across the country.

Our sins are grievous, but these Christians remind us that we are not yet beyond redemption. It is time to act on what we say we believe. We need to remember the words of the prophet Isaiah: "And they shall beat their swords into plowshares, and their spears into pruning hooks." We need to remember the words of Jesus—"Blessed are those who are persecuted for righteousness's sake"—and join the righteous cause of the protesters. For theirs is the kingdom of heaven.

LOOKING OUR RACIST
HISTORY IN THE EYE

An exhibit about the civil rights movement in Nashville
proves Faulkner was right: the past
isn't dead. It isn't even past.

SEPTEMBER 10, 2018

In 1960, the Reverend Dr. Martin Luther King Jr. gave a speech in this city, which was emerging as a training center for nonviolent protest. "I came to Nashville not to bring inspiration," he said, "but to gain inspiration from the great movement that has taken place in this community."

That movement was the work of people who later became some of the most influential figures in the national struggle for civil rights: James Lawson, John Lewis, Z. Alexander Looby, Diane Nash. When people today think of the civil rights era in the South, they think of Birmingham, Alabama. They think of Little Rock, Arkansas. They think of Forsyth County, Georgia, which warned African Americans passing through not "to let the sun go down on your head." They don't think of Nashville.

But this was the first major city in the South to desegregate public facilities, lunch counters, and movie theaters. It developed a calm, one-year-at-a-time approach to integrating city schools. When Ms. Nash, confronting Mayor Ben West, asked if it was wrong "to discriminate against a person solely on the basis of his race or color," Mr. West answered, simply, "Yes."

These are the stories Nashville tells itself again and again: we aren't like the rest of the South. Dr. King said so.

The problem with civic memory is that it is both true and deeply false. Some layer of reality inevitably undergirds a public fairy tale. A myth always contains enough truth to make it seem like the final word. But there's no such thing as the final word. That's because any history is a narrative construction, one that files off the roughest edges of the story. The past itself is shaggy, troubled, unruly. It will not be contained. William Faulkner said it best: "The past is never dead. It's not even past."

Here's what's true: Nashville did not attack its own children with fire hoses, as Birmingham did. Tennessee did not call out the National Guard to integrate its universities, as Mississippi did. There is no "Bloody Sunday" in our history, as there is in the history of Selma, Alabama. But our stories about the orderly desegregation of schools and the peaceful desegregation of lunch counters and the benign treatment of Black people by the white people in power? That's all a myth.

We Shall Overcome: Civil Rights and the Nashville Press, 1957–1968, an exhibit of photographs assembled by the Frist Art Museum, exposes such mythmaking for what it is. The collection features work by photographers at Nashville's two daily newspapers, *The Tennessean* and the now-defunct *Nashville Banner*, taken during the struggle for civil rights in the city. Very few of these images were published; only a handful were seen by people of the time.

Part of the collection is on display in the museum's ground-level public gallery, through which virtually all visitors pass. The full collection appears in a companion book just released by Vanderbilt University Press. The most troubling images appear only in the book. "As a mother of young children, I very conscientiously attempted to address the dark moments of the history, but without the images that may be viewed as most disturbing, especially for a family unprepared for what they were going to see or even participants in the movement who may still be traumatized by their experience," said exhibit curator Kathryn Delmez.

One 1957 photo depicts a crowd gathered in the middle of the night outside the newly integrated Hattie Cotton School, which had been bombed shortly before. A photo from 1960 shows the aftermath of a bomb set off at the home of Mr. Looby, an attorney who defended sit-in demonstrators in court. Another, from 1962, depicts the Reverend Cephus Coleman standing in front of his own house as it burns to the ground. Two 1963 photos show a girl—all of fifteen—lying unconscious in the street, beaten by a police officer with a club. In another photo from 1963, an effigy of Dr. King is hung by the neck in the headquarters of the Nashville police.

The civil rights era in Nashville, in other words, was "peaceful" only in the context of the even greater brutality of our neighbors to the south.

And to the north and west, too. People in other parts of the country like to imagine that their own histories contain nothing like the dark shame of racism that haunts the South, but that belief is also a myth. In 1964, the year the Civil Rights Act passed, there were protests and violence in Chicago; St. Augustine, Florida; Tulsa, Oklahoma; New York City; Rochester, New York; Philadelphia; and Jersey City. In Cambridge, Maryland, National Guard troops—bayonets drawn—surrounded Black people kneeling in prayer.

For some time now, Nashville's civic institutions have been issuing correctives to the persistent myth of peaceful integration here. The astonishing Civil Rights Room at the Nashville Public Library aims to tell the whole story of African Americans' struggle for full civil rights in Nashville. The nonprofit organization Historic Nashville offers a tour of civil rights landmarks in the city. In 2017, *The Tennessean* published a series of unvarnished stories about the conflicts of that time. In 2016, when Representative Lewis returned to Nashville to accept the Nashville Public Library Literary Award on the heels of winning the National Book Award for his graphic memoir, *March: Book Three*, the mayor gave him prints of his first police mug shots, taken after his arrest at the lunch counter sit-ins and long believed to be lost to history. In Nashville, we no longer want our ugliest moments to be lost to history.

The photography exhibit at the Frist closes October 14, but this record of Nashville's past will endure: copies of the show's companion volume will be distributed to all branches of the Nashville Public Library and to every public school in the city, and all members of the Tennessee General Assembly will receive a copy to deliver to the public libraries in their own communities. Here's hoping they pause to take a look first. There's a truth in these photographs that many of them have likely never seen before.

MIDDLE PASSAGE TO MASS INCARCERATION

*I thought I knew about the ubiquity
of racism. I was wrong.*

June 25, 2018

I went to Montgomery, Alabama, to visit the Legacy
Museum and the National Memorial for Peace and
Justice, two new spaces commemorating the history of
systemic racism in this country, but I didn't truly believe
they were meant for people like me. Surely they were
aimed at other people—white people who can't or won't
see the culture of white supremacy that surrounds them,
and Black people whose experience of this wrenching history has never been documented and ratified in quite this
way before.

I was wrong.

Montgomery was the first capital of the Confederacy
and the center of an immense domestic slave trade. The
Legacy Museum, which stands at the site where slaves were
imprisoned before being auctioned, follows history "from
enslavement to mass incarceration." The museum is compact, but its mix of meticulously researched displays—both
the high-tech (holograms of nineteenth-century slave and
twenty-first-century prison narratives) and the simple (a wall
of jars, each containing soil from the site of a documented
lynching)—offers a stark view of American history, from
slavery to segregation to persistent sentencing inequities

and voter suppression. It is nothing less than a narrative history of American racism.

The hallway leading from the museum's lobby to its first exhibit is a black tunnel that slopes downward to facsimiles of cells. Inside each one, holograms tell stories of life under slavery. "Mama?" one young boy calls into the darkness. You have to step close to the bars to hear him.

Another display is a seemingly everlasting slideshow listing some of the more than four thousand African Americans known to have been lynched between 1877 and 1950. Their "crimes" included refusing to run an errand for a white woman, asking a white woman for a drink of water, and rejecting a white man's bid for cotton seed. These lynchings weren't committed solely in the former states of the Confederacy, either: crowd-administered torture and execution also occurred in states like Ohio, New Mexico, Illinois, Kansas, Pennsylvania, and others. In 1920, three African American men were lynched before thousands of white people in Duluth, Minnesota.

If the Legacy Museum is an overwhelming immersion in careful data, the National Memorial for Peace and Justice, its companion space, is a direct blow to the gut. Both sites are the result of years of research by the Equal Justice Initiative, a legal nonprofit that works to end racial and economic injustice, particularly in connection with mass incarceration.

When the memorial, which occupies six acres at the top of a hill overlooking downtown Montgomery, opened in April, it received considerable national attention. But nothing I read prepared me for my own emotional response to it.

The centerpiece of the open-air site is a collection of more than eight hundred steel columns. Each is roughly the dimension of a coffin and designed to run with blood-colored rust in the rain. Each bears the name of an American county and the names and death dates of the victims who died violently there.

There is no ignoring how personal this history is. My grandfather was nineteen when two Black men named Juster Jennings and Sills Spinks were lynched in his Alabama county in 1920. I couldn't help myself: after seeing the column with their names, I had to look up the distance between the place where they were lynched and my grandfather's farm. I felt a perverse amount of relief when I realized it was almost certainly too far for him to have traveled by mule.

But I had to admit that I couldn't honestly say whether my grandfather would have wanted to be there. By the time I knew him, he treated everyone courteously. But he also asked my grandmother to stop teaching when Alabama schools were finally integrated. (She did not.) So I just can't say.

Here's the truth about the ubiquity of racism: I'm fifty-six years old, and there's a bleeding column in that memorial for every place I've ever lived.

The sheer numbers are devastating, but it's their placement that works most powerfully to convey the magnitude of loss. They are mounted at eye level as visitors first enter that part of the memorial, but as the floor slopes downward, the columns begin to rise. About halfway down the walkway, looking up and straining to read the engraved names, visitors suddenly realize that they are standing beneath a representation of bodies that have been hung from nooses and left to dangle there.

"God, they just go on and on," I whispered to my husband. A Black man standing nearby turned and looked at me. I couldn't read his expression.

Heading back toward Nashville on Interstate 65, I noticed a giant battle flag of the Confederacy flying on the side of the highway outside Verbena, just north of Montgomery. I could swear I'd never seen that flag before, though I grew up in Alabama and though I've driven the length of that state during each of the past four summers. I wondered if the flag's flagrant placement, so close to Montgomery, was an in-your-face rebuke to the presence of the Legacy Museum and the National Memorial for Peace and Justice.

Then I looked it up. Turns out the flag was raised in 2005 by the Alabama division of the Sons of Confederate Veterans. I just hadn't noticed it before.

IN MEMPHIS, JOURNALISM
CAN STILL BRING
JUSTICE

The nonprofit newsroom MLK50, founded by Wendi C. Thomas, aims to carry on the work that Martin Luther King Jr. started.

MAY 25, 2020

W endi C. Thomas launched MLK50 in 2017 as a one-year project to make the fiftieth anniversary of the assassination of the Reverend Dr. Martin Luther King Jr. a time to consider the current state of economic justice in the city where he was murdered while advocating for a living wage.

"Underpaid Black workers and their plight drew Dr. King to Memphis more than fifty years ago," Ms. Thomas said in a phone interview last week. "That's why he was here. And while I wouldn't say that Memphis has made no progress, it's hard to fathom that Dr. King would be proud of where we're at." In Memphis, almost 28 percent of the population lives in poverty, and that number is growing.

Ms. Thomas was under no illusion that simply telling the stories of underpaid workers, immigrants, and other vulnerable Memphians would sort out the economic issues that make it so difficult for them to emerge from poverty. "The city has made a commitment, a *commitment*, to low-wage industries, which means low-wage labor, which means systems that exploit, for the most part, Black and brown workers," she said. But telling their stories was a start. Three years later, her one-year project is still going strong.

Educated in Memphis schools, Ms. Thomas is a veteran journalist with more than twenty-five years of reporting and editing experience at daily newspapers in Indianapolis, Nashville, and Charlotte, North Carolina. For eleven years, she served as a columnist and assistant managing editor at *The Commercial Appeal* in Memphis. By the time she'd completed a year as a fellow at the Nieman Foundation for Journalism at Harvard University, she had both the knowledge and the experience to build a newsroom from scratch.

What she didn't have was funding. In the beginning, for weeks on end, she worked sixteen- and eighteen-hour days, living off her credit cards while building a news source unlike any other in Memphis. "We unapologetically exist to dismantle the status quo where it doesn't serve low-income residents in Memphis, the overwhelming majority of whom are Black," Ms. Thomas said. "We're not a Black publication, but we frame the news from the perspective of the most vulnerable."

Ms. Thomas's investigative series on predatory debt collection by a nonprofit hospital system affiliated with the United Methodist Church, the largest hospital chain in the Memphis area, revealed that these hospitals sued their own low-income employees for failing to pay their medical debts. In other words, a faith-based hospital system both failed to pay its employees a living wage and sued them for being unable to pay their bills. To add insult to injury, workers' health-insurance policies did not cover care at rival hospitals with more generous financial-assistance policies.

"Profiting from the Poor," written in partnership with the ProPublica Local Reporting Network, earned Ms.

Thomas an Investigative Reporters and Editors Award and the 2020 Selden Ring Award for Investigative Reporting, a prestigious prize from the Annenberg School at the University of Southern California. It also resulted in a revised hospital policy that forgave a staggering $11.9 million in medical debt.

In the three years since MLK50 launched, the publication has grown to include a managing editor, a visuals director, and a senior editor, and it hires a range of freelancers, all of whom are paid. Thanks to large grants from the American Journalism Project and the Racial Equity in Journalism Fund at Borealis Philanthropy, Ms. Thomas is now poised to expand her nonprofit newsroom to include a development director and an operations manager. A full-time Report for America corps member will join the team, as well.

MLK50's most recent recognition is a $72,420 grant from the Facebook Journalism Project to cover the coronavirus pandemic with a focus on Memphis's most vulnerable citizens. Working in collaboration with other local media outlets—the *Memphis Flyer, High Ground News,* and *Chalkbeat Tennessee*—MLK50 will use the funds to develop a text-messaging system to help disseminate crucial health information to people in areas of the city with limited internet access.

Despite these achievements, the office of Memphis's mayor, Jim Strickland, has refused to include MLK50 on the city's media-advisory list, through which officials communicate with journalists. In a lawsuit filed against the city earlier this month, Ms. Thomas argues that her exclusion from the list is both unconstitutional and a transparent act of retaliation for MLK50's critical coverage of the mayor's office. Ms. Thomas stands by her reporting. "They may not like what I write, but it's not wrong; it's not factually incorrect," she said on the phone. "My ethics and my commitment to fairness and accuracy are impeccable."

Ethics, fairness, accuracy, social justice reporting, journalists who hold elected officials to account—all of these public goods are harder and harder to come by these days. Newspapers have been in a state of crisis for decades. Between 1990 and 2016, some 60 percent of newspaper jobs in this country disappeared. Earlier this year, the McClatchy Company, publisher of thirty dailies, including *The Sacramento Bee* and *The Miami Herald*, filed for bankruptcy. And that was before the current pandemic accelerated newspaper losses across the country. BuzzFeed News has called the coronavirus "a media extinction event."

Such losses are particularly acute in places where no other media outlets are covering news that affects poor residents and where the government is not working on their behalf. And Memphis does not hold a monopoly on that combination of circumstances. "The South tends to have lost more papers, and have more counties without newspapers, than any other place," Penny Abernathy, a professor of journalism at the University of North Carolina, told *The New Yorker*'s Charles Bethea earlier this year.

Across the region, examples abound. As Lyndsey Gilpin, founder and editor of the nonprofit news site *Southerly*, noted in a report for the *Columbia Journalism Review* earlier this year, the proposed Atlantic Coast Pipeline, a massive fracking project with potentially devastating consequences to both the environment and human health, would disproportionately impact already struggling Southerners, many of whom live in counties without a single newspaper.

Wendi Thomas is as cognizant of these trends as anyone, but her experience as the founder of MLK50 gives her a perspective that offers hope: "We're in a moment where the future of journalism can look really grim, but it's also a moment when we can reimagine what we do," she said.

That hope is tempered by an awareness of economic vulnerability: "You have more time and more bandwidth to dream when you're not worried about where your next paycheck is coming from," she noted. "But if we can find some space to imagine what's possible, maybe we could make more progress in making our communities fairer for the people who have been pushed to the margins."

AN OPEN LETTER TO
JOHN LEWIS

*For being a moral compass for the nation, we owe the
congressman from Georgia, who is fighting a new
battle, our deepest gratitude.*

JANUARY 6, 2019

Dear Mr. Lewis, I write with a heavy heart. Stage 4 pancreatic cancer is a terrible diagnosis, so it's no surprise that last Sunday night the internet erupted with anguish as news of your illness became public. Treatment may give you a "fighting chance" to continue working "for the Beloved Community," as you wrote in a statement, but it's painful to think of what you will be called on to bear in the coming months. You have already borne so much for us.

In the National Civil Rights Museum in Memphis, a massive screen plays a montage of film and still photos from March 7, 1965, a day now commemorated as "Bloody Sunday." The images were made at the beginning of a planned march from Selma to Montgomery, Alabama's capital, to claim voting rights for the Black citizens of the state. I grew up in Alabama, not far from Selma, and I've always known the story of Bloody Sunday, but knowing the story is not the same thing as watching it unfold on a life-size screen. Standing in the National Civil Rights Museum on Martin Luther King Jr. Day a few years ago, I watched in horror. What you and your fellow marchers, 600 strong, found waiting for you on the other side of the Edmund Pettus Bridge were 150 state police and local law enforcement officers armed with billy clubs, bullwhips, and tear gas. They gave you two minutes to disperse.

As the chairman of the Student Nonviolent Coordinating Committee, you were standing at the very front of the march. You were wearing a light-colored trench coat, and that coat is what makes it possible to follow you in the black-and-white footage of those next chaotic moments. One minute and five seconds after the two-minute warning, evil advanced and the carnage began, even as you knelt in the road to pray.

The beating you took that day from an Alabama state trooper may have fractured your skull, but it didn't crack your resolve. National news stories carrying photos and film footage from Bloody Sunday finally woke this nation to what was happening in the Jim Crow South, and that awakening ultimately led to the passage of the Voting Rights Act five months later.

On that account alone your sacrifice will always be remembered. But what followed Bloody Sunday has been more than five decades of service to this country. During those years, your commitment to nonviolent protest has never wavered, not even through more than forty arrests and attacks, not even through too many reversals of hard-won gains.

"I have been in some kind of fight—for freedom, equality, basic human rights—for nearly my entire life," you wrote in the statement announcing your illness. "I have never faced a fight quite like the one I have now."

You may not have faced this particular fight, Mr. Lewis, but you have spent your life facing down a malignancy that has ravaged this country from its very founding. The racism that led you to the March on Washington in 1963 and to the foot of the Edmund Pettus Bridge in 1965 still rages in the body politic today. Indifference to the poor and the disenfranchised is still a hallmark of state government here in the South—and not just in the South. These are the battles you continue to fight as a United States congressman representing Georgia's Fifth District.

From a sharecropper's shack outside Troy, Alabama, where as a young boy you preached to the chickens, to the battlegrounds of the civil rights movement to the hallways of the federal government, you have been a moral compass for the nation and a voice for freedom and democracy in the world: leading a sit-in on the floor of the House of Representatives to demand a vote on sensible gun legislation, fighting for equitable health care for the poor, and just last month announcing the passage of a bill that would strengthen the Voting Rights Act.

It would be easy to lose heart at the rank nationalism and flagrant racism still on display in our own day. It's always tempting to give up in the face of the two-steps-forward-one-step-back nature of any fight for justice. But you have never given up, and you have never given in to despair.

In 2016, eight days after the presidential election, you won the National Book Award for the third volume of *March*, your graphic memoir for young readers. Two days later, you returned to Nashville, where you once were a student, to receive the Nashville Public Library Literary Award. The very highlight of my professional life is the interview you gave me in our library's beautiful Civil Rights Room—and surely the lowest point is the fact that tears ran down my face the entire time.

You were kind enough to pretend not to notice, but you offered some words of comfort, too: "In these days that seem to be so dark, I think the spirit of history is still leading us and guiding us—I believe in that. Call it what you may, but I believe that somehow, in some way, good is going to prevail. And out of some of the darkest hours, there will be daybreak. There will be light. And we will get there. You have to believe it. You have to believe in your guts that it's going to be OK."

We can't help leaning hard on your optimism, relying on the certainty of your hope. As you face the trials of cancer treatment, I hope you will feel surrounded by the love of all the people you have comforted over the years. A grateful nation is praying for you, Congressman. We are praying for your health and your courage. We are praying for your comfort and your peace. And we will never cease praying for your Beloved Community. We will never cease praying for this country to become the place you have always believed it could be.

READING THE NEW SOUTH

A group of forward-thinking, upstart journals and
websites are exploding the stereotypes so many
attach to this place and its people.

SEPTEMBER 17, 2018

I was a graduate student in Philadelphia when James Watt, the former Secretary of the Interior of the United States, came to campus in 1984. Mr. Watt's brief tenure in federal office was characterized by an almost cartoonish villainy. *Rolling Stone* called his attitude toward the environment a "rip-and-ruin view of our natural resources, land, water, parks and wilderness." That night, Watt argued for letting each state set its own air- and water-safety standards, a position that makes no sense if you're aware that rivers and winds don't stop at state borders.

During the Q and A, I took my turn at the microphone to make this point. "Sir," I said, "I'm from Alabama." Instantly that giant audience of Pennsylvanians broke into laughter. Who was this cracker daring to voice an opinion about federal environmental policy?

Well, that was 1984, you're probably thinking. Today we don't judge people by their accents any more than we judge them by their skin color. People know better now.

In fact they don't. The political polarization of our own day means that a region like the South, a red voting bloc in national elections, is a source of continual liberal ridicule, no matter the subject. In June, I wrote about the transcendently beautiful Mobile-Tensaw Delta, one of the most ecologically diverse places in the country. When I posted the link on Facebook with a note about its magic, someone commented, "Except that it's in Alabama." As though nothing in the whole state could possibly have any value.

As stereotypes go, this one surely doesn't rank among the top ten most objectionable human prejudices, but it stings even so. Fortunately there is plenty of on-the-ground proof to counter it. Among the most important is a raft of publications, many so new they're still on shaky financial footing, that aim to convey the genuine complexities of the modern American South. They are planted in the South and created by Southerners, people who love this place but who nevertheless see it all too truly.

Unlike lifestyle glossies like *Southern Living* and *Garden & Gun* (which is assiduously apolitical, despite what its name might suggest), these publications blast past sweet-tea-and-moonshine preconceptions to convey the nuances of a region where people are rarely as ornery or dumb as they're held to be in the national imagination.

The oldest of them is the *Oxford American*, founded in Oxford, Mississippi, but now based in Little Rock, Arkansas, which was first launched in 1992. (A print quarterly, it has foundered a number of times over the years, ceasing publication until new funding arrived, which somehow always has.) In many ways, it set the tone for all the publications that followed, celebrating the artistic innovations of the region but refusing to gloss over its manifold shortcomings.

The latest issue includes a nonfiction report by Kelsey Norris on a Nashville oral history project focusing on the descendants of slaves; Beth Macy's profile of the Appalachian playwright and novelist Robert Gipe; "Bikers," a poem by the Virginia native Kate Daniels about her brothers ("What foreign lives they lived / With their deer hunts, and their / Love of speed, and their boring jobs / In factories"); and a short story by David Wesley Williams about a hitchhiker stuck in West Memphis, Arkansas. The story is called "Stay Away from Places with Directions in Their Names."

The tagline for *Facing South*, an online publication of the progressive Institute for Southern Studies in Durham, North Carolina, is "A Voice for a Changing South." The site focuses on politics, history, and human rights, with recent articles on voting rights during Reconstruction, South Carolina's present refusal to evacuate convicts in advance of Hurricane Florence, and delays in compensation for people sickened by the 2010 Deepwater Horizon disaster in the Gulf of Mexico.

Scalawag, another nonprofit publication out of Durham, also reports regional politics with a progressive eye, though it covers regional art and literature, too, and includes a section titled, simply, "Witness." The magazine, which is published online and in print, fosters "critical conversations about the many Souths where we live, love, and struggle" and aims to empower "activists, artists, and writers to reckon with Southern realities as they are, rather than as they seem to be." Recent stories confront toxic masculinity, explain how to fight racism through the auspices of craft beer, collect a range of Latinx poetry from around the American South, and report on Syrian cuisine in small-town Georgia.

The Southern Foodways Alliance, based in Oxford, Mississippi, publishes a print quarterly called *Gravy*. Despite its name, the journal does more than report on cuisine, continuing the work of the alliance itself by showcasing, through food, "a South that is constantly evolving, accommodating new immigrants, adopting new traditions, and lovingly maintaining old ones." The latest issue includes an article on "The Queer Pleasures of Tammy Wynette's Cooking" by Mayukh Sen and a profile of Joe Stinchcomb, an African American bartender who invented five new cocktails to celebrate Black History Month. The drinks had names like "Blood on the Leaves" and "(I'm Not Your) Negroni," and they definitely raised some hackles down there in Mississippi.

For anyone still hoping to define Southern literature, *storySouth* is an online literary journal based in Greensboro, North Carolina. It publishes "the best fiction, creative nonfiction, and poetry that writers from the new south have to offer," according to its website. Subjects that seem to play into regional stereotypes can be found there at times. The current issue features a poem called "Roadkill" by Megan Blankenship and one by William Woolfitt called "Grassy Branch Pentecostal Church, Face of Christ on Tin," for example. But read the poems: this is not your unlamented Agrarian's Southern literature.

Perhaps the liveliest of the whole bunch is an absolutely wonderful online publication called *The Bitter Southerner*, an irreverent Atlanta-based site that truly covers the cultural waterfront, celebrating the lunacy of genuine homegrown geniuses, lifting up the unsung heroes of the region, and peeking behind the veil of great cultural institutions, all while holding power to account in a part of the world where power has too often lost its uneducated mind.

But it's the newest of these publications that most often captures my own attention these days. *Southerly* began in late 2016 as a weekly newsletter of investigative journalism, plus curated links to "News Flying Under the Radar" by other journalists around the region. Until this summer, when it received a grant from Solutions Journalism Network, it was funded entirely by Patreon subscribers, who monthly contribute an average of five dollars each through an online portal. Those supporters are still crucial to its survival. Lyndsey Gilpin—the magazine's founder, editor, and publisher—is a Northwestern University–trained journalist based in her hometown, Louisville, Kentucky, and her weekly reports from impoverished and often oppressed corners of the South have given a microphone to people whose voices are rarely heard in conversations about climate change, environmental exploitation, or economic disparity.

In July, *Southerly* grew into a full-fledged "independent media organization" that "covers the intersection of ecology, justice, and culture in the American South," according to its new website, and already it is taking no prisoners. The site—in partnership with *The Montgomery Advertiser* and *Scalawag*—launched with a four-part series on the breakout of tropical diseases in the rural South owing to failing sewage infrastructure. On September 22, *Southerly* will convene a public discussion in Hayneville, Alabama, about poverty-related illnesses and how communities can address the governmental crisis that spawned them.

Southerly's mission statement sets out some uncompromising goals: "This region stands to bear the brunt and lose the most from the effects of climate change. It is experiencing massive economic shifts from a changing energy industry. The South is the fastest urbanizing area of the U.S., but it is also the most economically distressed. Southerners deserve a publication that covers the nuances of their environment, history and communities without being condescending or stereotypical, without parachuting in from large metropolitan areas. The rest of the world deserves to know about the creative ways communities here are adapting to these changes, and the challenges that come with that."

You could almost call it a mission statement for celebrating—and transforming—the South itself.

THESE KIDS ARE DONE WAITING FOR CHANGE

*In less than a week, six Nashville teenagers created a
march that drew ten thousand peaceful protesters
and gave hope to a whole city.*

JUNE 15, 2020

In real life, Nya Collins, Jade Fuller, Kennedy Green, Emma Rose Smith, Mikayla Smith, and Zee Thomas had never met as a group when they came together on Twitter to organize a youth march against police violence. It was unseasonably hot, even for Middle Tennessee, with rain predicted. Earlier protests here had ended in violence, with the Metro Nashville Courthouse and City Hall in flames. Collectively, these are not the most promising conditions for gathering a big crowd, much less a calm one. But the teenagers were determined to press on, even if hardly anyone showed up.

On June 4, five days later, the founding members of Teens for Equality—as the young women, ages fourteen to sixteen, call their organization—were leading a march of protesters some ten thousand strong, according to police estimates. "I was astonished," Kennedy Green, fourteen, told me in a phone interview last week. "I did not know there were that many people in Nashville who actually see a problem with the system. I was like, 'Oh, my gosh, there are so many people here who actually care.'"

The protesters, most in their teens and twenties, chanted "Black lives matter" and "No justice, no peace"

148

and "Not one more" as they marched for more than five hours. There was not one hint of disarray in their ranks, no angry confrontations with National Guardsmen or police officers clad in riot gear.

"As teens, we are desensitized to death because we see videos of Black people being killed in broad daylight circulating on social media platforms," said Zee Thomas, fifteen, in a speech that opened the march. "As teens, we feel like we cannot make a difference in this world, but we must."

They already have. The march they organized—with advice from the local chapter of Black Lives Matter—was one of the largest protests against white supremacy in Nashville history. Mayor John Cooper has responded to the protests by announcing that Nashville police officers will begin wearing body cameras next month. The cameras have been long planned and also long delayed, despite strong public support amid an increasingly frayed relationship between the police department and many of the communities they serve.

When these Teens for Equality look around them, what they see is the strength in their numbers and the power of their own voices. Those of us who are long past our own teen years have watched powerful social movements rise and fall. We have seen hard-earned social change walked back by new leaders. We might be forgiven our despair that anything in this magnificent, damaged country will ever change.

But the protests that have risen up in the wake of George Floyd's killing show every sign of being different. Across the country they have continued unabated, bringing change astonishingly quickly. Readers in large numbers are moving to educate themselves about systemic racism—in just a few weeks, demand for books about the topic has surged. White Americans are finally taking a hard look at policing practices in their communities and changing their opinion about the Black Lives Matter movement. Police departments are taking a hard look at themselves, too, banning chokeholds and other life-threatening methods of restraint. This time, "a glorious poetic rage," as the Minneapolis author and activist Junauda Petrus-Nasah put it, is finally changing the country for good.

The recent protests, Kennedy Green says, have turned her into an optimist: "I mean, when have all fifty states ever done anything together? And all fifty states have marched because of the death of George Floyd and for the Black Lives Matter movement. I do believe in the future because there are a lot of kids who are changing the future, trying to end white supremacy and hatred and racism in America."

This optimism is founded in more than one hugely successful march. It's also founded in data: new polling shows that 80 percent, or more, of American adults ages eighteen to twenty-nine support Black Lives Matter.

Nya Collins, Jade Fuller, Kennedy Green, Emma Rose Smith, Mikayla Smith, and Zee Thomas are not alone. They belong to a long tradition of youth activists that includes the Children's Crusade of the American civil rights movement; the anti-war activists of the Vietnam era; the Pakistani women's education activist Malala Yousafzai; the gun-control activists Emma González, David Hogg, and other survivors of the massacre at Marjory Stoneman Douglas High School in Parkland, Florida; the Indigenous Canadian clean-water activist Autumn Peltier; and the Swedish climate activist Greta Thunberg, just for starters.

These young people are passionate about their causes and unwavering in their commitment to change. The world they have inherited is deeply troubled and desperately flawed, and they see with clear eyes both the errors of earlier generations and the hope of their own. Their power lies in the undeniable moral authority of youth: they did not cause the mess they have inherited, but they are rolling up their sleeves to clean it up.

Above all, they are brave, enduring withering attacks by craven adults who hold no scruple against threatening children. You may argue that these activists are simply too young to understand the risks they are taking, but I think they know exactly what they are doing. What they are too young for is cynicism. What they are too young for is defeat.

They are young enough to imagine a better future, to have faith in their own power to change the world for good. And that faith should give the rest of us more hope than we have had in years.

ENVIRONMENT

AMERICA'S KILLER LAWNS

Homeowners use up ten times more pesticide per acre
than farmers do. But we can change
what we do in our own yards.

MAY 18, 2020

One day last fall, deep in the middle of a devastating drought, I was walking the dog when a van bearing the logo of a mosquito-control company blew past me and parked in front of a neighbor's house. The whole vehicle stank of chemicals, even going forty miles an hour.

The man who emerged from the truck donned a massive backpack carrying a tank full of insecticide and proceeded to spray every bush and plant in the yard. Then he got in his truck, drove two doors down, and sprayed that yard, too, before continuing his route all around the block.

Here's the most heartbreaking thing about the whole episode: he was spraying for mosquitoes that didn't even exist. Last year's extreme drought ended mosquito-breeding season long before the first freeze. Nevertheless, the mosquito vans arrived every three weeks, right on schedule, drenching the yards with poison for no reason but the schedule itself.

And spraying for mosquitoes isn't the half of it, as any walk through the lawn-care department of a big-box store will attest. People want the outdoors to work like an extension of their homes—fashionable, tidy, predictable. Above all, comfortable. So weedy yards filled with wildflowers get bulldozed end to end and replaced with sod cared for by

155

homeowners spraying from a bottle marked "backyard bug control" or by lawn services that leave behind tiny signs warning, "Lawn care application; keep off the grass."

If only songbirds could read.

Most people don't seem to know that in this context "application" and "control" are simply euphemisms for "poison." A friend once mentioned to me that she'd love to put up a nest box for bluebirds, and I offered to help her choose a good box and a safe spot for it in her yard, explaining that she would also need to tell her yard service to stop spraying. "I had no idea those guys were spraying," she said.

To enjoy a lush green lawn or to sit on your patio without being eaten alive by mosquitoes doesn't seem like too much to ask unless you know that insecticides designed to kill mosquitoes will also kill every other kind of insect: spiders and mites, honeybees and butterflies, native bees and lightning bugs. Unless you know that herbicides also kill the insects that ingest the poisoned plants.

The global insect die-off is so precipitous that, if the trend continues, there will be no insects left a hundred years from now. That's a problem for more than the bugs themselves: insects are responsible for pollinating roughly 75 percent of all flowering plants, including one-third of the human world's food supply. They form the basis of much of the animal world's food supply as well. When we poison the bugs and the weeds, we are also poisoning the turtles and tree frogs, the bats and screech owls, the songbirds and skinks.

"If insect species losses cannot be halted, this will have catastrophic consequences for both the planet's ecosystems and for the survival of mankind," Francisco Sánchez-Bayo of the University of Sydney, Australia, told *The Guardian* last year.

Lawn chemicals are not, by themselves, the cause of the insect apocalypse. Heat waves can render male insects sterile; loss of habitat can cause precipitous population declines; agricultural pesticides kill land insects and, by way of runoff into the nation's waterways, aquatic insects as well.

As individuals, we can help to slow such trends, but we don't have the power to reverse them. Changing the way we think about our own yards is the only thing we have complete control over. And since homeowners use up ten times more pesticide per acre than farmers do, changing the way we think about our yards can make a huge difference to our fellow creatures.

It can make a huge difference to our own health, too: as the Garden Club of America notes in its Great Healthy Yard Project, synthetic pesticides are endocrine disrupters linked to an array of human health problems, including autism, ADHD, diabetes, and cancer. So many people have invested so completely in the chemical control of the outdoors that every subdivision in this country might as well be declared a Superfund site.

Changing our relationship to our yards is simple: just don't spray. Let the wildflowers take root within the grass. Use an oscillating fan to keep the mosquitoes away. Tug the weeds out of the flower bed with your own hands and feel the benefit of a natural antidepressant at the same time. Trust the natural world to perform its own insect control, and watch the songbirds and the tree frogs and the box turtles and the friendly garter snakes return to their homes among us.

Because butterflies and bluebirds don't respect property lines, our best hope is to make this simple change a community effort. For twenty-five years, my husband and I have been trying to create a wildlife sanctuary of this half-acre lot, planting native flowers for the bees and the butterflies, leaving the garden messy as a safe place for overwintering insects. Despite our best efforts, our yard is being visibly changed. Fewer birds. Fewer insects. Fewer everything. Half an acre, it turns out, is not enough to sustain wildlife unless the other half-acre lots are nature friendly, too.

It's spring now, and nearly every day I get a flyer in the mail advertising a yard service or a mosquito-control company. I will never poison this yard, but I save the flyers as a reminder of what we're up against. I keep them next to an eastern swallowtail butterfly that my ninety-one-year-old father-in-law found dead on the sidewalk. He saved it for me because he knows how many flowers I've planted over the years to feed the pollinators.

I keep that poor dead butterfly, even though it breaks my heart, because I know what it cost my father-in-law to bring it to me. How he had to lock the brakes on his walker, hold on to one of the handles, and stoop on arthritic knees to get to the ground. How gently he had to pick up the butterfly to keep from crumbling its wings into powder. How carefully he set it in the basket of the walker to protect it.

My father-in-law didn't know that the time for protection had passed. The butterfly he found is perfect, unbattered by age or struggle. It was healthy and strong until someone sprayed for mosquitoes, or weeds, and killed it, too.

DANGEROUS WATERS

*The Tennessee River is one of the most ecologically
diverse rivers in the world. It is also
one of the most polluted.*

OCTOBER 29, 2019

F rom a distance, a river looks less like a feature of the terrain than like a massive, mysterious animal. A river is
a sleek, writhing being, and even the verbs we use to
describe it evoke animation. A river runs through it. A river
climbs its banks. A river empties itself into the sea.

Rivers and creeks run through the American South as
bountifully as veins and arteries run through the human
body, and are just as necessary for life. For the peoples native
to this part of the world, these rivers were a source of food,
water, and transport, and almost all the early European set-
tlements in the South were founded next to rivers, too, and
for the same reasons. The rich soil of a river floodplain is
ideal for planting, and in times of drought, the river is the
farmer's savior. For enslaved people, and later for the tenant
farmers who were effectively enslaved, access to a river
could mean the difference between living and starving:
anyone who could catch a fish would not go hungry.

The great river of my own life is the Tennessee, which
separates the place where I live from the place where I grew
up. The river is more than 650 miles long, and its watershed
is the fifth largest in the nation, encompassing parts of six
bordering states, as well as Tennessee itself. Crossing the

Tennessee River in northern Alabama means I am heading home, no matter which direction I'm driving.

The last three months have been an uncommon season of travels for me, and this river has often been my companion. I have seen it from the sky on the way to St. Louis and again on the way to Minneapolis. I have driven alongside it in Chattanooga and Knoxville. I have crossed it in Alabama and crossed it again, without seeing it, while driving white-knuckled through the remnants of Hurricane Barry in west Tennessee.

In all those places the Tennessee River is beautiful. Trees in a thousand shades of green and gold edge its banks, a patchwork quilt made entirely of leaves and pine needles. On windy days, whitecaps flicker on its placid surface. In the Appalachian foothills, limestone bluffs rise high above it, a cross section of time itself. It is one of the most ecologically diverse rivers in the world—what Anna George, vice president of conservation science and education at the Tennessee Aquarium, calls "an underwater rain forest."

It is also one of the most polluted rivers in the world. A study announced earlier this year found that the level of microplastics in the Tennessee River is among the highest ever measured. These particles are known to accumulate in the gills and stomachs of ocean fish, and to move up the food chain when a larger fish eats a smaller one. There are far fewer studies on the impact of plastics in freshwater ecosystems, but early investigations suggest that the same principles apply. And we are the creatures at the top of the food chain.

But it's not just plastic. Through the auspices of the Tennessee Valley Authority, the Tennessee River system is the reason much of the Upper South finally gained access to electricity, but TVA has not always been a good steward. In

2008, one of the worst environmental disasters in the history of this country occurred near Kingston, Tennessee, when a holding pond's dike broke, spilling a billion gallons of toxic coal ash into waterways that drain into the Tennessee River. More than a decade later, TVA is still storing coal ash in unlined pits and ponds that leach heavy metals into the groundwater and ultimately into the river.

And for the past year Chelsea Brentzel, a reporter for WHNT News in Huntsville, Alabama, has been investigating a story so outrageous it would be unbelievable if it weren't taking place in the context of these other environmental degradations: for nearly a decade, the 3M Company's plant in Decatur, Alabama, illegally released toxic chemicals into the Tennessee River with the full knowledge of the Alabama Department of Environmental Management. The practice, which Ms. Brentzel's reporting helped to end, came to light only because dangerous levels of those chemicals were found in the area's drinking water.

Driving south on I-65, just past the Tennessee border, an Alabama welcome center boasts a full-size Saturn rocket pointing into the sky, a nod to the US Space and Rocket Center in nearby Huntsville. The rest stop also features a stone monument to sheer Southern cussedness. The carving reads, "ALABAMA: WE DARE DEFEND OUR RIGHTS," the state's official motto. But in terms of environmental protections, the state motto of Alabama is nothing more than a terrible lie.

We know how it happened. It happened because this is what always happens when "business-friendly" politicians take the reins of government. The Trump administration is currently rolling back environmental protections in every imaginable federal context—forests, waterways, air quality, endangered species—and, in a rich irony, moving to limit states' rights to establish more stringent environmental protections of their own. As for the rapidly unfolding global climate emergency, the Trump administration doesn't believe in the rapidly unfolding global climate emergency.

Many organizations are working hard to insert the law between this wrecking ball of a government and our only inhabitable planet. Led by California, nearly two dozen states are suing the federal government to protect the right to set their own vehicle-emissions standards. Another coalition of states and cities is suing to block the administration's rollback of Obama-era restrictions on carbon dioxide emissions by coal-burning power plants. Last week, on behalf of eleven conservation organizations, the Southern Environmental Law Center filed a legal challenge to the administration's repeal of major provisions of the Clean Water Act.

The only thing that will truly reverse these life-threatening, science-denying policies is the collective will of the American people. It will require all of us, whatever our politics, to force our government to protect our birthright. Preserving our oceans and rivers should not be a partisan issue. Protecting the land that sustains us should not be a partisan issue. Protecting the air we breathe should not be a partisan issue. And it's up to us to defend our rights because these are our rivers, and these are our skies. And this planet is our home.

MORE TREES,
HAPPIER PEOPLE

*When cities grow, green space dies. Replanting it has
been shown to lift the human spirit.*

OCTOBER 7, 2018

The scene in a pocket park outside Plaza Mariachi on
Nashville's Nolensville Pike last Wednesday was
like a tableau from a Norman Rockwell painting,
twenty-first-century style. Surrounded by signs advertising the
Hispanic Family Foundation, Dubai Jewelry, the Dominican
Barber Shop, and restaurants offering Peruvian, Chinese,
Mediterranean, and Indian food—as well as a GameStop
franchise and H&R Block—was a sign that read, "Today.
Free trees."

The arrow on the sign pointed to a pop-up canopy where
the Nashville Tree Foundation was hosting its fourth tree
giveaway of October. A family standing under the canopy
was posing for a photo with the sapling they had just adopted.
Carolyn Sorenson, executive director of the foundation, was
taking the picture: "Say 'trees'!" she said.

The tree giveaway at Plaza Mariachi happened to fall on the
day that Nashville's mayor, David Briley, announced a campaign
to restore and enlarge the city's tree canopy. The effort, called
Root Nashville, will be overseen by the city and the Cumberland
River Compact, an environmental nonprofit, and funded
through a combination of public, corporate, foundation, and
private dollars. Together with several municipal departments

and other nonprofit organizations, the initiative aims to plant five hundred thousand trees in Davidson County by 2050.

Many of these newly planted saplings will replace very large, very old trees that have been lost to Nashville's meteoric growth—a population increase of more than 45 percent since 2000. As the city has grown, the city's trees have fallen: deliberately felled by developers to make room for new construction or unintentionally killed as a side effect of nearby building. Just since 2008, the tree canopy in the urban core has dropped from 28 percent to 24 percent, a loss of roughly nine thousand trees a year.

The Nashville Tree Foundation's giveaway program—which continues through Friday—is just one of the group's outreach efforts, each focused on planting trees in the poorer parts of town, which tend to have the least green space. "We're all working toward the same goal of five hundred thousand trees, and we want an equitable distribution of free trees in the county," said Ms. Sorenson. "We usually plant in areas where there's an intersection of low canopy and low income. We're trying to make a large impact over a short period of time."

I learned about the tree giveaway through social media. That's also where I heard Erica Ciccarone's story of the developer who cut down three ancient black walnut trees on the property line they share. What's going up next to Ms. Ciccarone's house in the Wedgewood-Houston part of Nashville is a four-story duplex, and she wasn't surprised when the builder took out the old tree closest to the monstrous structure under construction. But there was no reason to take down the trees in the back of the lot.

As it happens, Ms. Ciccarone lives in an area where the tree canopy is well below its target density, but for her the loss of the black walnuts was personal. "They weren't majestic," she wrote in an email. "Their leaves were small and scraggly. But they provided shade for us and the chickens, housed songbirds, and they blocked the sight line from the alley into our yard and back porch."

Her reaction is typical: When trees die, people invariably mourn. And when trees are planted, people become demonstrably happier. Rhitu Chatterjee of National Public Radio recently reported on a randomized study designed to discover the effect of urban green space on mental health. The study found that cleaning up vacant lots and planting grass and trees were associated with a significant improvement in the mental health of nearby residents: according to the study, "feelings of depression and worthlessness were significantly decreased."

An earlier experiment by Eugenia South, one of that study's authors, found that merely walking past a newly planted lot in an urban neighborhood lowered the participants' heart rates. Unrelated studies have found lower blood pressure readings and lower cortisol levels among participants who spent time in nature.

From an urban planning perspective, trees do something of the same thing for densely occupied parts of the planet. They remove carbon, including greenhouse gas emissions, from the air. They cool the surrounding area, offsetting the heat impact of asphalt and combustion engines. They absorb and filter stormwater. They lower energy costs for nearby buildings. It's no wonder that so many people in Nashville are worried about their trees.

When I left Plaza Mariachi last week, Ms. Sorenson was taking a photo of another family and the oak tree they had just selected for their yard. The father was holding the heavy tree, which was taller than his little girl's head. Dressed in *Where's Waldo?* stripes, she was lifting her hands toward it anyway, reaching high, wanting to help.

I HAVE A CURE FOR THE DOG
DAYS OF SUMMER

*It's hot, the pandemic is still raging,
and did I mention that it's hot?*

AUGUST 10, 2020

A ugust and February are the two months I like least.
August because it's hot and dry and the wildflowers
are mostly spent. February because it's cold and gray
and by February I have lived too long without wildflowers.
Owing to climate change, February doesn't get all that cold
anymore, though it's still gray. February will always be gray in
Middle Tennessee.

And August will always be hot. Sweltering hot. Heat-
rising-in-shimmering-waves-above-the-pavement hot. Drink-
straight-from-the-hose hot. February-is-starting-to-look-pretty-
good hot.

They're called the dog days, but not for the reason everyone thinks. Yes, dogs do spend August lying around in the
shady dirt, panting. Dogs can't sweat where they have fur,
and they can't take off their fur coats. It would make sense
for "dog days" to be a reference to the way dogs turn into
puddles of lassitude during August.

Alas, no. "Dog days" refers to Sirius, the Dog Star, which
in late July rises in the sky just before the sun does. The
ancients believed the Dog Star ushered in a time of drought
and madness, a time when people are apt to start wars or hurl
insults on Twitter.

167

Here in the dog days of the pandemic summer, fear and fury are now deeply embedded in my psyche. I am furious at the "leaders" who have failed to contain this virus, and I am fearful for the safety of everyone I love.

Next week, my sixty-one-year-old husband will return to teaching teenagers, a population not known for successful social distancing, and our youngest son will head back to college, where he will join a population that is neither good at social distancing nor supervised by anyone who is. Our middle son now holds a job that requires him to travel, often by air, for at least part of every week. Our oldest son and brand-new daughter-in-law are sick with Covid at this very moment—a mild case, knock on wood, but you know how a mother worries.

I try to remind myself that I am not alone in these creeping fears. Everyone I know is trembling, worried, anxious. Now in the pandemic's sixth month, we've felt like this for so long it's begun to seem like the way it has always been and the way it always will be. I know that's not true with my conscious mind, but my 3:00 a.m. mind is louder than my conscious mind, and these days it's 3:00 a.m. all the time.

My own cure for a darkness that never lightens is to head outdoors. Except for calls of nature, my little rescue dog prefers not to join me in this heat. She appears to believe that the dog days of summer are meant to be the dog days of air-conditioning. No matter. There is more to see without her.

August is spider season, a time when the baby orb weavers that spent all summer hiding from predators have grown large enough to spin a web. At dawn, the silken threads are beaded with drops of water, as bright as any diamond. In the pollinator patch, the milkweed pods are on the verge of bursting, sending white feathered seeds wafting on the wind like snow, and the pokeweed berries, too, are beginning to ripen, turning dark purple against magenta stems. All manner of songbirds flutter beneath each dangling cluster, harvesting berries on the wing. From a distance it looks as though the whole plant is on the verge of levitation.

My coneflowers have lost almost all their petals by now, and the goldfinches have picked the cones free of seeds, but the black-eyed Susans are still in full golden glory. The asters and goldenrod are just getting started, and the zinnias are almost as tall as I am, brightly colored and showy enough for a butterfly to see from high in the air. I've been worried about the butterflies this year. I planted a whole new bed of nectar and host plants to fill the sunny space left where we lost a maple tree last spring, but until last week the butterflies themselves were almost entirely absent.

Was it because of my neighbors' pesticides? The ten-day warm spell last winter? The cool, wet spring? I don't know why, but the only butterfly I saw for weeks was a lone eastern tiger swallowtail. Where were the fritillaries and the sulfurs and the little hairstreaks? Where were the question marks and the cabbage whites and the common buckeyes? Where oh where were the monarchs?

Finally, a painted lady arrived, followed by a clouded sulfur. A gulf fritillary showed up the same day as a monarch—they got into a swirling orange tussle over ownership rights to the zinnias before moving to separate parts of the flower bed. I'm hoping the monarch will stay around long enough to lay eggs on the milkweed, and the gulf fritillary will lay her eggs on the passionflower. I planted those flowers just for them.

One day it was all skippers—several silver-spotted skippers and a gorgeous fiery skipper—and the next it was all swallowtails. I love the swallowtails almost as much as I love the monarchs. But I have imperfect vision and struggle to tell a dark-morph eastern tiger swallowtail from a black swallowtail from a spicebush swallowtail, especially in flight. Last weekend, as I was squatting to get a closer look, I was startled to see at least a dozen tiny yellow-and-black-striped caterpillars on the parsley I planted in case a black swallowtail needed it for a nursery. And, look, here were the baby swallowtails themselves!

At that is how, deep in the summer of our national terror, I learned to love August: because the heat and humidity of the dog days dispelled the 3:00 a.m. darkness and brought the butterflies back to me at last.

THE CASE AGAINST
DOING NOTHING

Taking a fatalist approach to climate change—or anything
else—merely plays into conservative hands.

OCTOBER 14, 2019

I f you're reading this, you're probably among the
Americans who don't get their news from conserva
tive echo chambers, so you've probably made some
changes in your habits of late. Chances are you feel pretty
good about them. You won't save the planet all by yourself, or make the country a more equitable place, but, hey,
doing something is always better than doing nothing.

You're covering your leftovers with beeswax wraps instead
of plastic, and you never drink from a straw anymore. You're
skipping the Roundup and pulling the weeds in your garden
instead. You're careful about how you use pronouns, making no
assumptions. You're writing to your elected officials to demand
affordable health care and sensible gun laws and a humane
immigration policy and full enfranchisement of your fellow
citizens. You're giving as much as you can to advocacy organizations that work full-time to protect the environment, the poor,
the victims of prejudice, the rights of women.

There's also a good chance that every single time
you've made one of these changes, someone you know,
someone who shares your concerns, has informed you that
such changes are not enough. Someone has looked at the
brand-new hybrid in your driveway and wondered why you

didn't go for the fully electric vehicle instead. Someone has looked at your fully electric vehicle and informed you that the power company in your area still relies in part on fossil fuels. Someone has seen the solar panels on your roof and informed you that you've undone all the good of those panels merely by taking that business trip to London. Haven't you heard what air travel does to your carbon footprint?

You mention at dinner that you've switched to grass-fed beef, and someone at the table will inform you that anyone who's truly concerned would have given up meat entirely. You switch to organic produce, and someone will remark on how organic farming will never be efficient enough to feed a growing population, and it does nothing to address the problem of food deserts in poor communities, either. You comment enthusiastically that the dryer balls you're using have really cut down on the amount of time—and thus energy—it takes to dry your clothes, and someone superior to you is bound to observe that a clothesline would work just as well and use no energy at all.

And if you've made all these efforts to make the world a bit better? Every last one of them? It won't matter. The scoldings will continue because personal efforts, as everyone knows, will not reverse the course of climate change. Personal advocacy, it is clear to anyone paying actual attention, will not undo the pernicious effects of voter suppression in red states or the rate at which President Trump is reversing environmental protections or the fact that Republicans have stolen a Supreme Court seat and politicized the institution itself. Besides, merely talking about it is nothing but virtue signaling.

"You know this is a drop in the bucket, right? You know this won't ultimately change anything." If I had a dollar for every time someone has made this point to me, I could buy out the fossil fuel companies myself and have money left over to retrofit the entire country in sustainable energy from sea to shining sea.

These "helpful" comments, in real life and on social media, aren't wrong. Personal efforts to combat any of the massive problems facing our environment, our culture, our very humanity, will inevitably fall short. Will using dryer balls shorten drying time and thus save energy? Yes. Will using dryer balls prevent global environmental collapse? No, it will not. But here's the real point: Will not using dryer balls help the world more than using them? Also no.

It's true that emphasizing individual responsibility runs the risk of letting people off the hook too quickly, that the satisfaction of doing something right can make it all too easy to ignore everything else they're getting wrong. Do-gooder complacency can be as much a risk as I-don't-even-notice-race racism or climate-change-is-a-hoax ignorance.

But shaming people for trying to do something good is just mean. Aren't we tired yet of all the cruelty already poisoning the air we breathe? More to the point, shaming someone for trying to do something good is no way to inspire more goodness. Despair, far more than an unrealistic hope, is the great danger we face today. If these small efforts do no good, what's the point of doing anything at all?

Doing nothing—to reverse climate change, to create a more equitable society, to elevate the marginalized, and to heal the sick—is exactly what the other side is already doing. Doing nothing is exactly what the climate deniers, the Koch network, the NRA, the fossil fuel industry, and every self-important legislator in every gerrymandered district in this country wants us to do as well. It doesn't matter whether the reason we're doing nothing is because we just don't care, or because we think it won't make any difference in the end.

Despair is paralyzing, and we have no time left for paralysis. Many small efforts, especially when amplified by those of others, can have a big effect. What if every home-owner in the entire subdivision stopped using poisons and planted a pollinator garden? What if all the neighborhoods in a city, in a state, in the nation, did likewise? These efforts alone are unlikely to save the pollinators—on whom so much of our farming, and thus our lives, depends—but they are the first steps toward the kind of collective consciousness raising that can be leveraged into political will.

Maybe it sounds like pie-in-the-sky Pollyannaism even to hope for such a thing, but hope is not a thing we can risk dismissing anymore. Until next year's election, at least, hope seems to be all we've got.

PLANTING SEEDS
IN SNOW

Letting nature take its course is getting harder to do.

FEBRUARY 26, 2021

Last week I started my garden in the middle of an ice storm. Sleet and snow poured down while I trudged out to the toolshed to fetch the seeds I'd saved from last year's pollinator patch. Still, it was time.

Light is brightening the sky earlier every morning, and lingering longer every afternoon, and the songbirds are already pairing off. The winter flock of neighborhood bluebirds has dispersed, leaving just one male and one female at the mealworm feeder each morning. All around the yard the downy woodpeckers and the Carolina wrens and the tufted titmice are traveling from branch to branch, two by two. They are just getting to know each other, I think. It's a little too early yet for actual nest-building.

It's also too early to plant seeds in the garden, but I don't sow these seeds in the soil. I start them in trays and store the trays in our refrigerator. For the next eight weeks, the seeds will lie dormant in an artificial winter.

This isn't always a necessary step. In the bright days of April, just as the ruby-throated hummingbirds are arriving here from their wintering grounds, I'll plant the cosmos and marigold and zinnia seeds straight into the flower beds. They will grow with hardly any effort on my part, almost regardless of the weather. A marigold seed will set down roots in turned soil if all you do is spit on it.

But some seeds need to endure a certain amount of cold before they can germinate, and our winters are getting warmer, random ice storms notwithstanding. I let my flowers go to seed to feed the birds, who are half the reason I planted this pollinator garden in the first place. But I always collect a few seeds from each variety to store in our toolshed. In late February, I bring the cold-dependent ones indoors to enjoy the steady coolness of our refrigerator, just to be safe.

The Deep South, where I grew up, has never had particularly cold winters, but the Upper South is different. Here, our growing seasons are tuned to both the heat of Southern summers and the cold of Midwestern winters. During my first January in Nashville, more than thirty years ago, I woke up in the middle of the night to brightness and thought it was morning. When I looked out the window, the trees were sweatered in white, sending a pale light into the room. I thought I'd moved to the most magical place in the world. Magnolias, just like at home in Alabama, and snow, too!

Back then we could count on several snows every winter. What we get now is less predictable and often the worst of both worlds: unseasonable mild spells that trick the songbirds into pairing off too soon, that trick the sap into rising in the trees and the woody shrubs and the perennial flowers, but also brutal cold spells that can wipe out many of my plantings—and many songbirds, too—in one nine-degree night.

In most matters of coexistence with the natural world, letting nature take its course is the right thing to do. If I see a rat snake climbing the cherry laurel, I'm obliged to let the snake go on its way, knowing it will eat the baby redbirds hidden in a nest deep in the greenery. If a red wasp is eating the gulf fritillary caterpillars on the passionflower vines that I planted just for them, there is nothing to be done about it. Nature's wisdom is still wise, even if it's painful to watch.

It's another matter altogether when a natural system encounters an unnatural hitch. I've installed snake baffles below all my nest boxes because a birdhouse doesn't have the camouflage of a nest hole in a dead tree. I owe it to the birds I've invited into my yard to protect them from the predators I know are here.

But the difference between what is part of a natural system and what is a human-introduced disruption is becoming less and less clear.

I put up these nest boxes because developers keep cutting down trees to make room for bigger houses, and every year there are fewer nesting places for the wild creatures that were here first. I planted this pollinator garden because the weedy flowers that once grew in the unkempt yards and rough margins between the houses of this formerly working-class neighborhood no longer have any place in the manicured yards of what my neighborhood has become.

Improving the survival odds of wildflower seeds by letting them winter in my refrigerator, unnatural as that may seem, is my way of responding personally to an unstable climate. It comforts me to know that I'll be able to replenish the milk-weed stands I've planted for the monarch butterflies, even if the recent storms have decimated my flower beds.

Nature did not design milkweed to be planted by human hands. Once the seedpods burst open, the seeds enter the world on their own miniature parachutes to be wafted away on the wind. In commercial packages, milk-weed seeds come denuded of their flight gear, but the seeds I save from my own flowers still have the gossamer filaments nature gave them, and they escape into my kitchen on the slightest breath.

I grieve what is happening to the natural world, and I understand perfectly well that my own efforts to help are far from enough. But when I watch a bluebird introducing his mate to the nest box I've installed for them, it's impossible to give up. When the tiny hummingbirds make it back from far across the Gulf of Mexico, it's impossible to give up.

And a seedling muscling through the soil, carrying its old, sleeping self into the light, never fails to give me hope. It never, never, never, never fails.

THE FOX IN THE STROLLER

It's human nature to tame wild animals, but nothing
in nature wants to be a pet.

APRIL 8, 2018

Being the caretaker of two very old dogs means frequent visits to the pet-supply store, but I don't take my geriatric companions with me when I shop. In their sore, deaf, rickety old age, they are made anxious by the bounding puppies in the store's cavernous fluorescence. For my dogs, a pet supermarket is a chamber of tortures.

And not only for them. I recently crossed the main aisle just as a big man pushing a stroller was coming the other way. The screen covering the stroller was zipped, and the animal inside had scooted back as far as it could, so I caught the barest glimpse of it. "That dog looks just like a fox," I said.

"It *is* a fox," the man said.

I squatted for a closer look. The creature inside drew back further still, but I could see it well enough to know it truly was a fox.

The man must've read the shock in my eyes because he immediately volunteered that he owned the fox legally, having bought it as a kit from a licensed breeder. This fox, a male, was skittish, he said, but his family also owned an arctic female who was friendly with strangers. Standing in line a few minutes later, I saw him leaving with a woman pushing a white fox in an identical stroller.

I've seen many foxes in the wild—and heard their unnerving screams in the dark—and I was sure the man was breaking the law. But I was wrong.

It's illegal here in Tennessee to remove any animal from the wild to keep as a pet, but wild animals raised in captivity are a different matter. With proof that the animal came from a legal source, it is indeed permissible to keep a captive-bred fox as a pet, as long as it doesn't belong to a species native to Tennessee. The fox in the stroller looked like a full-blooded Tennessee gray fox to me, but he must have been some other state's fox.

"Taming" a wild animal is merely the act of desensitizing it to human beings, and the temptation to do it seems hard-wired into us. In high school I taught a backyard squirrel to climb into my lap and take shelled pecans from my fingers. Last summer, I would whistle for the bluebirds every time I filled the mealworm feeder, and they would fly to the nearest branch and wait impatiently for me to step away. To anyone watching, it must have looked as though I had a pet family of bluebirds, and in truth it would have been no great trick to move my chair closer and closer to the feeder until those birds were eating from my hand. But doing that would have been an unkindness.

Few animals in the wild can tell the difference between the person who feeds them and any random person in the same vicinity. My tame squirrel used to startle my mother by creeping up and licking her toes while she hung laundry on the line—he seemed to be unaware of the difference between toes and fingers and hoped she came bearing pecans, too. That kind of confusion is why a tame animal can easily be mistaken for rabid by people who don't know it's tame. It's why "pet" animals in the wild are often euthanized.

And orphan animals raised by humans are the most vulnerable of all, unprepared to live in the wild, if they even survive a clueless rescuer's attempt to feed them.

As a college student in Alabama, I was trained as a wildlife-rescue volunteer. I raised many orphaned animals—rabbits, squirrels, opossums, songbirds—and released them according to a protocol designed to give them the best chance at survival. These days, if I find an injured bird or an orphaned squirrel, I take it to Walden's Puddle, the wildlife rehabilitation center closest to me.

And yet all over social media, I see images of cute baby animals being reared by well-meaning people who have found a cottontail rabbit's nest and assumed the babies were orphaned, or fledgling birds they assumed had fallen from the nest. In most cases, the babies are fine and the anxious parents are nearby, just waiting for the bumbling humans to leave them alone.

These wild animals may eventually be tamed, but they'll never be domesticated. A tamed animal might seem affectionate, but it maintains all the normal propensities of its species, and its offspring will not exhibit any inherent friendliness toward humans—the babies will need to be tamed all over again. Domesticated animals, by contrast, have been selectively bred for human companionship across thousands of years.

It's possible to domesticate foxes, as Russian scientists in Siberia have proved—a story fascinatingly told by Lee Alan Dugatkin and Lyudmila Trut in *How to Tame a Fox (and Build a Dog): Visionary Scientists and a Siberian Tale of Jump-Started Evolution*. But it takes many generations to do so. Some offspring don't exhibit the traits of domesticated animals despite nearly seventy years of selective breeding.

I sympathize with the desire to bring wild animals into the human sphere. Every spring, I sit outside near the safflower feeder in the sun of a Sunday afternoon, as still as I can manage, and a tufted titmouse will invariably land in the tree next to me, hopping closer—limb to branch to deck rail to chair back—until finally she is sitting on my head. I thrill to feel her tiny passerine claws scrambling against my scalp. I try not to yelp when she yanks out my hair to line her nest.

But the best way to love a wild animal is to leave it in the wild, a world that coexists with our own but is always apart from ours. I can't shake the image of that fox in the pet store—its lowered head and averted eyes, the intelligence of its ears, the delicate precision of its paws. What a magnificent animal, revered since the earliest days of human culture for its cleverness and wiles. What a terrible fate, to be zipped up in a nylon stroller and wheeled between the electric fences and the rhinestone collars.

DEATH OF A CAT

*For weeks, I have been trying to understand my own
tears in the presence of a dying creature I did not love.*

AUGUST 3, 2020

I first saw it in bits—two paws here, the tip of a tail there—
on grainy, black-and-white images taken by our backyard
trail camera. Normally that device captures only the wild
animals you'd expect to find in a first-ring suburb: opossums,
mainly, but also rabbits and raccoons and rat snakes, sometimes an owl, now and then a fox. I once saw a bobcat slink
across our street, but it's never shown up in the trail-cam photos. My heart lifted when I first saw a clearly feline haunch in
one of the pictures, but the scale was all wrong for a bobcat. It
was just an ordinary house cat, prowling in my backyard.

Soon the cat was showing up in the daytime, too,
apparently drawn by the lunch remains left around the construction site two doors down from our house. He was a
ragged, battle-scarred tom, thin but not emaciated, with
one eye that didn't open all the way. A feral cat, not someone's cherished pet.

As we passed my husband's car in the driveway one
morning, my skittish rescue dog darted away from the tires,
spooked by something under the car. I squatted down for a
look. The feral cat hissed at me.

Let me just say it, flat out: if I owned a gun, I swear I
would have shot that cat. I would have chased that hissing cat
out from under the car without a thought and shot it as it fled.

I wish you could see all the baby birds in our yard. Baby towhees and robins, baby redbirds and bluebirds. Two broods of house finches and two broods of house wrens. One morning, an ungainly fledgling crow sat nearby and rustled its feathers, yelling for food like a giant nestling. A fuzzy screech owl chick spent an entire day staring wide-eyed at me from a tree near our back deck while its mother dozed beside it.

We've had baby downy woodpeckers and red-bellied woodpeckers, baby white-breasted nuthatches and northern flickers. All summer long, they have been taking their wobbly maiden flights from branch to fence post, from cherry laurel to holly hedge. They try to land on the birdbath and miss altogether. They fly to the ground to catch an insect and then can't figure out how to take off again.

Our bug-averse neighbors poison every crawling or flying thing in sight, but my husband and I have spent years trying to make a haven here for wildlife, including the insects that pollinate flowers and feed reptiles and birds. Maybe you can picture these adorable baby birds and this flowering, insect-friendly yard. If so, you might forgive me for losing my mind a bit when the feral cat showed up.

I was thinking of the first nest the bluebirds built this spring, the one in which not a single baby survived. I was thinking of the gravid broadhead skink who would lie on our stoop every afternoon, warming her egg-swollen body in the sun. She disappeared one day to lay her eggs and guard her nest, I assumed, but now I wasn't sure. I was thinking of the chipmunk who lives in a tunnel under our stoop and of the screech owl, its feet holding down some small prey, its eyes glowing in the infrared light of our trail camera.

The more I thought about those vulnerable creatures, already crowded out by construction and starved out by insecticides, the angrier I got at the feral tom. In truth, I would never kill a cat, but I can surely hate one with a murderous rage.

Cats are domestic animals that don't belong outdoors. In the natural world, including my own backyard, animals kill one another every day, but there is ample scientific evidence that predation by cats is not part of any natural order. "House cats have a two- to 10-times larger impact on wildlife than wild predators," Roland Kays, a zoologist at the North Carolina Museum of Natural Sciences, said earlier this year.

The effect is even more devastating with feral cats, descendants of house cats that are not socialized to human beings: in Australia, feral cats have already been the driving force in the extinction of twenty-two species. From an eco-logical standpoint, the domestic cat, whether feral or a free-range pet, is an invasive species, every year killing billions of birds and mammals already imperiled by habitat loss, pesti-cides, and climate change.

The morning after I didn't kill the feral cat, a child from the neighborhood came to get me, hoping I could help a sick cat she'd found in her family's driveway. A few weeks earlier, this child had taken an infant deer mouse out of her dog's mouth, and I had kept it alive overnight, long enough to drive it safely to Walden's Puddle, a wildlife rescue organization. There it would be raised with other baby mice and then set free to fulfill its role in the natural cycle of things. My young friend was hoping for another miracle.

There would be no second miracle. When we got to her house, the embattled tomcat was lying in the driveway, his limbs twitching, his eyes unseeing, his hindquarters resting in a pool of urine. From time to time his neck would arch, and his mouth would pull back in a grimace. Our feral cat was in agony. Our feral cat was dying, and his suffering broke my heart.

Later, when animal control picked up his body, we learned that the cat had been poisoned. Most likely a neighbor had set out rat poison, and the cat had caught and eaten a dying rodent.

Cats are killers, but they are not apex predators. In this neighborhood, there are coyotes, great horned owls, and at least one camera-shy bobcat. Any one of them could handily kill a cat, but our feral cat didn't lose his life to a hungry owl or coyote or bobcat. He died because a human being was too squeamish to set the kind of trap that leaves behind a corpse to dispose of. There are mousetraps that kill quickly and painlessly, and those traps don't weaponize the mouse, turning it into a poison-delivery system for predators, but such traps do require people to face what they are doing: taking the life of another creature.

For weeks I have been trying to understand my own tears in the presence of a dying cat I did not love. It's hard not to feel connected to a living thing in a state of suffering. In "Death of a Pig," E. B. White writes, "He had evidently become precious to me, not that he represented a distant nourishment in a hungry time, but that he had suffered in a suffering world." I understand that essay now.

In the weeks since the tomcat's terrible death, I have thought a lot about the danger outdoor cats pose to the natural world and also about the danger the natural world poses to cats. Most of all I have been thinking about the way human beings, the deadliest predators of all, keep finding new ways to destroy everything that sustains the planet that sustains us. A hungry animal cannot be faulted for killing to eat. A feral cat—like a house cat allowed to roam outdoors—is not an evil creature. Like the poisoned mouse and the poisoned insects and all the other animals crowded out by development, it is simply a creature that has been failed by human beings.

My young neighbor came to me for help. At ten years old, she was sure that someone my age would know what to do about a dying cat. I did not know what to do, and I couldn't tell her that the true miracle would not have been the saving of a doomed cat's life. I couldn't tell her that the true miracle will never come until human beings have finally learned to live a better way: in concert with the natural world, and not in domination.

A 150,000-BIRD ORCHESTRA
IN THE SKY

*A huge flock of purple martins is using Nashville as a
staging ground for the fall migration—and bringing
music back to the city's shuttered symphony center.*

SEPTEMBER 7, 2020

A t first they circle high in the evening sky. But as night
descends, they, too, begin to descend, bird by bird,
one at a time, and then all in a rush: 150,000 purple
martins swirling together, each bird calling to the others in
the failing light as they sweep past the tops of buildings in the
heart of downtown Nashville. To anyone watching from the
ground, they look like one great airborne beast, one unmistak-
able, singular mind.

Their music grows louder and louder as the circles
tighten and the birds swing lower and lower, settling in the
branches of sidewalk trees, or swerving to take off again as
new waves of birds dip down. They circle the building and
return. They lift off, circle, reverse, settle, lift off again. Again
and again and again, until finally it is dark. Their chittering
voices fall silent. Their rustling wings fall still.

It is not like Hitchcock: watching these birds is nothing
at all like watching crows and seagulls and sparrows attack
the characters in *The Birds*, his classic horror film. The purple martins that have been gathering here during the past few
weeks are merely doing what purple martins always do this
time of year: flocking together to fatten up on insects before

making the long flight to South America, where they will spend the winter.

That's not to say the birds aren't causing problems. The place where they have chosen to roost this time is Nashville's Schermerhorn Symphony Center, which was already having a terrible year. With all scheduled programming canceled or postponed by the pandemic and so much of the symphony budget based on ticket sales, the organization had no choice but to furlough all the musicians and most of the staff and hope for better days. What the Nashville Symphony got instead of better days was a plaza full of bird droppings and elm trees so burdened by the weight of 150,000 birds alighting in them night after night that whole limbs are now bent and hanging limp.

The folks at the Schermerhorn at first assumed the birds roosting in their trees were starlings. Downtown Nashville is home to a large number of European starlings that live here year-round, and they have been a nuisance in years past. It's easy to mistake a flock of purple martins for a flock of starlings, especially when actual starlings join the martin flock from time to time.

Starlings are an invasive species, introduced during the early 1890s by Shakespeare enthusiasts determined to bring to the United States every bird ever mentioned in Shakespeare. All two hundred million starlings now living in North America are descended from a few dozen birds unwisely released into Central Park during the late nineteenth century. Thanks to the Migratory Bird Treaty Act, it is against the law to kill native songbirds. It is perfectly legal to kill starlings.

The transcendently beautiful Schermerhorn is built of limestone, which is highly porous. "The sheer amount of bird poop was causing a massive amount of damage," my old friend Jonathan Marx, the interim chief operating officer of the Nashville Symphony, said when I called him to ask about the purple martins. "But we never had any intention of killing the birds. We just wanted them to move on." The plan was to disperse them by fogging the trees with grape-seed oil.

Purple martins have been roosting in the Nashville area for years—at least since 1996, according to Melinda Welton, the conservation policy co-chair of the Tennessee Ornithological Society—though always before in much smaller numbers. Among birders, word quickly got around that the purple martins had settled in at the Schermerhorn this year, and in far, far greater numbers than ever before. "It's a pretty remarkable roost—definitely one of the larger ones in the country," Joe Siegrist, the president and chief executive of the Purple Martin Conservation Association, said on the phone last week.

Which is why Kim Bailey, Kim Matthews, John Noel, Anne Paine, Ms. Welton, and Mary Glynn Williamson went into action as soon as Mr. Noel noticed a pest control truck on the symphony plaza. It was, as Mr. Marx put it, "a collision of people who are taking care of their property with people who are staring in awe and wonder at the birds."

Purple martins are already in trouble from virtually every angle imaginable. Climate change has intensified hurricane season, making the fall migration even more perilous. Deforestation has destroyed the birds' natural nesting sites, and aggressive nonnative species like starlings and house sparrows have claimed most of those that remain. Like other swallows, purple martins are insectivores, but pesticides have made food scarce. One reason the birds chose Nashville as their migration staging ground may be its proximity to the insect-rich Cumberland River.

That night, while Ms. Bailey, who works as a staff naturalist at the Warner Park Nature Center, explained to the exterminators that purple martins are a federally protected species, others in the group starting calling and texting and messaging everyone they could think of who might be able to help: NewsChannel 5, the mayor's office, the Tennessee Wildlife Resources Agency, and local conservation nonprofits like the Tennessee Wildlife Federation, the Nature Conservancy in Tennessee, and the Nashville Wildlife Conservation Center.

Those folks reached others, who in turn contacted others still. With phones ringing and emails flying and social media on fire, the exterminators hastily decamped. The group stayed put, Ms. Bailey told me in an email, until they received assurances from a TWRA officer that he had contacted the pest control company and the truck would not be returning that night.

And now, like a flock of purple martins, this story veers in an unexpected direction. A tale of conflict becomes instead the story of human beings who listened to one another and then came up with a plan that would benefit everyone involved, and the birds most of all.

Mr. Marx heard from a number of conservation groups that evening and others the following day. Each time, he explained that the symphony staff believed they were hosting purple martins and, now that they knew the truth, would never harm or harass the birds. But he also pointed out that the flock had already caused significant property damage: the cost of power-washing the front of the building alone is at least $10,000, and that's not even addressing the rest of the building or the damage to the trees.

"As soon as we heard that, we started trying to think of ways in which we could work together," Terry Cook, the state director for the Nature Conservancy in Tennessee, told me. "One, we wanted to mitigate the current impact of the roost, but, two, we wanted to think about long-term opportunities to either make the site less preferable to purple martins in future years or to embrace this as a unique Nashville event."

Within hours, the Tennessee Wildlife Federation and the Nature Conservancy in Tennessee had joined forces to start a fundraising campaign to help with cleanup costs. "In the conservation community, we felt like we needed to rally around this problem so the symphony wouldn't have to carry this burden alone," said the Tennessee Wildlife Federation's Kendall McCarter, who hosts a nesting colony of purple martins in his own yard every year. "Especially right now, when they're in a very difficult place because of Covid."

The initial campaign to pay for power-washing the Schermerhorn's facade was fully funded within hours, but the appeal is ongoing, and any extra money it raises will be used to treat damage to the trees, to replace trees that can't be saved, and to help with costs that arise during future purple martin migrations. Because the birds, which seem to prefer well-lighted roosts, will most likely be back.

In one way of looking at it, this rescue operation mimics the long relationship between human beings and purple martins themselves: even as we are responsible for the birds' troubles, we are also responsible for their survival. The population east of the Rocky Mountains, where 98 percent of all purple martins live, "is completely reliant on people putting up birdhouses for them to reproduce in," said Mr. Siegrist. "If people didn't do that, the bird would go extinct in the majority of its range. Each one of those birds putting on that spectacular display in downtown Nashville exists because people cared enough to put up a birdhouse. Each one of those birds came from somebody's backyard."

"We're so thankful to have community partners who are willing to help us deal with this completely unexpected situation," said Mr. Marx, "because we need to be putting our focus on the fundraising that's going to allow us to bring our musicians back to work. This is a time when so many people are under so many forms of duress, but one thing we know is that music is one of those things that brings people together."

Until then, this collaboration between naturalists and the symphony is, for everyone involved, a happy ending at a time when people are desperate for happy endings. "I'm so excited about how it's been handled there in Nashville," Mr. Siegrist said. "I think it can be a blueprint for other communities."

I find myself dreaming of a time when the musicians of the Nashville Symphony are back in that beautiful space, perhaps even playing a sunset concert, the doors of the Schermerhorn thrown wide to the music of purple martins swooping down from the sky. What a glorious sound that would be, after this year of silence and fear. What a gift to gather together and hear that music—the music our own species makes and the music of the birds. Both at once.

FAMILY
& COMMUNITY

WAKING UP TO HISTORY

*At new museums, the past is finally becoming more
than the story of men and wars.*

APRIL 1, 2019

Like many girls of my generation in the rural South, I learned every form of handwork my grandmother or great-grandmother could teach me: sewing, knitting, crocheting, quilting. I even learned to tat, a kind of handwork done with a miniature shuttle that turns thread into lace. Some of my happiest memories are of sitting on the edge of my great-grandmother's bed, our heads bent together over a difficult project, as she pulled out my mangled stitches and patiently demonstrated the proper way to do them.

But by the time I'd mastered those skills, I had also lost the heart for them. Why bother to knit when the stores were full of warm sweaters? Why take months to make a quilt when the house had central heat? Of what possible use is tatting, which my great-grandmother sewed to the edges of handmade handkerchiefs, when Kleenex comes in those purse-size packages?

But my abandonment of the domestic arts wasn't just pragmatic. By the time I got to college, I had come to the conclusion that handwork was incompatible with my own budding feminism. Wasn't such work just a form of subjugation? A way to keep women too busy in the home to assert any influence in the larger world? Without even realizing it, I had internalized the message that work traditionally done by men is inherently more valuable than work traditionally done by women.

I came to this unconscious conclusion almost inevitably. When every history class I ever took featured an endless list of battles won and lost by men, of political contests won and lost by men, of technological advances achieved by men, it's not surprising that the measure of significance seemed to be the yardstick established by men—almost exclusively of white men.

Public history has the power to affect our understanding of reality. It tells us what we should value most about the past and how we should understand our own place within that context. Just as art museums today must wrestle with an earlier aesthetic that excluded women and artists of color, local-history museums are working to recalibrate the way they present the past.

In Montgomery, Alabama, the Legacy Museum and the National Memorial for Peace and Justice convey the history of systemic racism in this country. In Louisiana, the restored Whitney Plantation's new focus is the way the enslaved people on the plantation lived. In Atlanta, the Cyclorama—a 360-degree diorama the length of a football field that depicts the Battle of Atlanta—was restored and returned to public display, this time with new interpretive materials that defy the Lost Cause myth. And in Memphis, the Pink Palace Museum has just opened an elaborate new exhibition, two years in the making, that celebrates the city's two-hundred-year history as a kind of web in which specific issues like race thread through seemingly unrelated categories like art and entertainment, commerce and entrepreneurialism, and heritage and identity.

Here in Nashville, the new Tennessee State Museum, which opened last October, addresses the history of the state in a new building whose design reinforces the idea that history is the story of everyone, of all the people. Andrew Jackson has his space, of course, but so do the Native Americans whom Jackson sent off on the Trail of Tears, a genocidal march out of their homeland. All the relevant wars are here, along with all the relevant weaponry, but so are the pottery shards and the bedsteads and the whiskey jugs and the children's toys. It's all arranged in a timeline that unfolds at a human pace and on a human scale, equally beautiful and inviting, informative and embracing. My people are from Alabama, not Tennessee, but this space feels as though it belongs as much to me as to any Tennessean because it tells the kinds of stories that could be the story of my people, the kinds of stories that earlier versions of public history had always deemed unworthy of celebration or scholarly attention.

As it happens, the museum's first temporary exhibition, which opened in February and runs through July 7, is a gallery full of gorgeous quilts. That was the exhibition I most wanted to see, and it did not disappoint. The quilts were made by familiar patterns—star and flower garden and log cabin and wedding ring—if not by familiar hands. Some of my own family quilts are gorgeously complex, but others are barely more than plain rectangles sewn in a row. I once asked my mother about those serviceable but hardly beautiful quilts, and she said impatiently: "People were cold, Margaret. They were trying to stay warm."

The quilts in the exhibition at the Tennessee State Museum would keep people warm, but they are also absolute showpieces, with carefully coordinated colors and tiny stitches so perfectly close together and so perfectly uniform that it seems impossible for them to have been made by human hands. These women were nothing less than artists, and the gallery's informational placards elevate them to that status and place them within that context. I studied the stitches and thought again and again of the women who had taught me to sit before a table frame and push a needle through all three quilt layers, taking stitches small enough to keep the batting from wadding up in the wash.

At the foot of our bed is a cedar chest that holds my share of the family quilts. The maple-leaf quilt was made for my childhood bedroom, but some of the squares were pieced together decades before I was born. The Sunbonnet Sue was my mother's baby blanket. The flower-garden pattern with the yellow border was the last quilt my great-grand-mother pieced by hand. My grandmother made the fan quilt for my husband and me when we got married. Shot through that quilt are memories—patchwork remnants of the dresses my mother made for me as I was growing up, bits left over from the simple blouses and skirts I made for myself in middle school.

Most of the older quilts were pieced by my great-grand-mother and quilted by the women of her Lower Alabama farming community, including my mother and grandmother, but others were given to my great-grandfather in payment for his services as a country doctor. If they couldn't afford his fee, his patients gave him what they could spare: a basket of eggs, a bag of pecans, a family quilt. In that way, another family's history—salvaged parts of worn-out clothes and bed-sheets—has become a part of my own family's history, and of your history, too, if you're reading these words. And that's exactly as the thinking behind the new history museums would have it.

WHY I WEAR FIVE
WEDDING RINGS

The women in my family made it possible
for me to face life's hardships.

NOVEMBER 24, 2019

Whenever I'm nervous, I find some sort of amulet to drop into my pocket. A buckeye. A feather molted from a blue jay's tail. The river rock my middle son always called a "worry stone." The spent egg sac from a praying mantis. A seashell from my mother-in-law's grave. I hold on to what's in my pocket the way an anxious baby clings to a beloved blanket at bedtime.

When I was about to give my first talk at a gathering of English teachers, my department head tried to reassure me. "Rule number one: don't sweat the small stuff," she said. "Rule number two: it's all small stuff."

That was more than thirty years ago, and I've lived long enough now, and buried enough loved ones, to know that in fact it's not all small stuff. Yet I still find myself fixating on matters that are indeed very small: the fancy wedding for which I have no suitable clothes, the thank-you notes I should've written by now. And the worst, by far, is the prospect of standing in front of a microphone.

Last summer, facing the first book tour of my life, I understood that no seashell or blue feather would carry me through two dozen events. I needed a security blanket more potent than any I'd ever before clutched in my sweaty hands.

Then, for reasons that aren't at all clear to me—reasons that in retrospect feel like an outright miracle—I thought of the family wedding rings.

Seven years ago, in the hospital where my mother was suddenly dying, I took the wedding band from her finger and slipped it on my own. At first it was simply a way to keep the ring from being lost in the shock and tumult of unplanned grief. But I've continued to wear it, year after year, because it means what a wedding band is supposed to mean. Like the ring my husband gave me thirty-one years ago, it's a reminder of love and fidelity—of my parents' unshakable love for each other, but also of their love for me, as reliable as any immutable force.

I'm the keeper of other family rings: my great-grandmother's, my grandmother's, my mother-in-law's. From time to time I would take them out to ponder for a moment, but I had never thought to wear them. Along with my mother, these women are at the heart of the memoir that was about to send me out on a book tour, and one day it finally dawned on me that their wedding rings would make the perfect talismans against fear. They would remind me that worry is pointless, that fretting about my own shortcomings as a public speaker will not make me a better public speaker. I took out the wedding rings of all my treasured forebears and put them on.

In what might be another minor miracle, for we are clearly in the realm of magical thinking here, it worked. I stood in front of microphone after microphone, spinning the thin bands around and around my fingers, and I looked out upon all those strangers, and, lo, I was not afraid.

Full disclosure: it's possible that menopause, which has fostered an "Oh, who in hell really cares?" attitude in me for some time now, may have dispensed with my lifelong stage fright, too, and I just never noticed, having been on no stages in recent years. But I prefer to think the family matriarchy saved me, that my beloved elders closed ranks around me, my mother and mother-in-law on one flank, my grandmother and great-grandmother on the other, to shore me up and give me strength.

I think of them again in this season of family gatherings, when heirloom recipes and holiday decorations are time capsules. I fiddle with their rings, which I'm still wearing, and remember the women who taught me what it means to face genuine hardship.

I give thanks for my great-grandmother, Ollie Mims, whose steadfast faith and unflinching calm got her through the Great War, the Great Depression, World War II, and countless family losses, including the death of her own son. I give thanks for my grandmother, Mildred Weems, who taught in a two-room country schoolhouse because my grandfather's farm never quite paid the bills. When the schools in Lower Alabama finally desegregated and everyone she knew, including my grandfather, urged her to retire, she ignored them all. "A child is a child," she said and kept on teaching.

I give thanks for my funny, creative mother, Olivia Renkl, whose laugh was so infectious that friends and strangers alike would laugh out loud in response, never suspecting the depressions she had endured all her adult life. I give thanks for my mother-in-law, Marie Moxley, who raised six children and still welcomed me into the family as a full daughter. For eighteen years she weathered Parkinson's disease without a word of complaint, setting an example of dignity, forbearance, and love that no one who knew her will ever forget.

Every family history includes such stories of survival, of prevailing against great suffering and despair. Perhaps these family histories, personal and utterly invisible to the world, hold the key to facing our larger worries, too, and showing the way through.

"Your hand feels just like your mother's hand," my father would tell me when I was still young enough to be holding his hand but already old enough to be growing into a woman's hands. I look at my hand now, my mother's ring on my finger, and I know what he meant. My hand is broad now where hers was broad, wrinkled where hers was wrinkled, and the same knuckles are just beginning to swell.

DEMOLITION BLUES

*Nashville's building boom has reached the place where
my family and friends wove a life.*

MARCH 18, 2018

T here's a mechanized tyrannosaur biting a hole in the
roof of my mother's last house. It moves hesitantly,
lifting its heavy head and widening its serrated
jaws before clamping down, then nosing around a bit,
finding purchase between bites, backing up and moving
forward to accommodate its long reach, its powerful orange
neck swinging right and left to bump walls that stubbornly
refuse to fall. I stand at the edge of the yard and watch the
house reduced to rubble.

The house stood directly across the street from mine—I
could see it from the window of my home office—but I almost
missed the demolition. Between the nail guns of the framing
crew five doors down and the blaring radio of the masonry
crew on the other side of the street, more than half the house
was gone before I even noticed. You would think the noise
of a whole house falling into dust would make an instant
impression, but I have lived with so much construction noise
in this neighborhood, and for so many years, that I've gotten
good at tuning it out.

There's a particular kind of heartbreak that comes of
watching a beloved neighborhood change so radically that
every house on the street has been scraped from the land, but
the heartbreak of this particular neighborhood is in no way

tied to issues of historic preservation. The original houses here were small brick rectangles, less attractive than a nice double-wide mobile home. Built after World War II for working-class servicemen buying on the GI Bill, each house followed one of two simple floor plans (or their mirror images), with slight variations—a covered stoop on some, a gable on others—to make them distinguishable from each other.

When my husband and I moved here in 1995, we had a young son and a baby on the way. Back then, there were only a handful of young families on this block. Most houses were still occupied by the original postwar couples aging in place, or by couples buying starter homes. As families grew, they mostly moved away, and a new young couple would move in to take their place.

It's a neighborhood of old shade trees, and we live on a quiet street with no through traffic, a place where, when our boys took their first solo rides on two-wheeler bikes, all the dog-walking and stroller-pushing neighbors would cheer them along their route, helping them up after the inevitable crash and comforting them till one of us could catch up on foot. Is it any wonder that my husband and I refused to move away, even after our second child, and then our third, was born? Even after my father got sick and my parents began to spend most of their time here with us?

Our friends in the neighborhood were having the same conversations as their own families grew, making much the same choices. We would close in the garage, add a room off the back, dormer the low attic and lodge an air conditioner into the sole window—anything to keep from leaving our friends. My husband and I added on twice: a family room after our third child was born, an extra bedroom when my father was sick. One of our older neighbors would stand in the street and watch these modest amendments underway, shaking his head: "There y'all go again, driving up my property taxes." When he moved to a condo a few yards outside the county line, a single mom with an infant promptly bought his house.

Over the years, our neighborhood became uncommonly close. Our children roamed in packs, our dogs drank from each other's water bowls, our holiday caroling ended in copious glasses of wine and children hyped on Christmas cookies and insufficient supervision.

The scale of the original houses meant that if a couple divorced, it was almost always possible for one of the parents to buy the other out, which meant the kids could stay here with us, part of a neighborhood-wide support system during a season of change. Older neighbors died, and we prayed at their funerals and checked on their grieving spouses as the seasons unfolded for them alone. When my mother was no longer able to live on her own, it seemed like nothing less than providential that the rental house across the street from us became available just as we were learning that she could never afford an assisted-living facility. Here, she didn't need one. We all assisted her.

In time "adding on" came to mean extensive whole-house makeovers with second stories and two-car garages. When it became clear that these seventy-year-old houses were already crumbling, unsuited for renovations on such a scale, my neighbors began to tear their own houses down. If you want more room and don't want to move—and if property values have grown so high that moving makes less sense—why not tear a wobbly old house down and move in with your parents while a nice new house rises in its place?

I hate living in a construction zone, but I love my neighbors, and I am always relieved when a family I love decides to stay.

But a decade ago, I didn't understand that when our oldest neighbors began to die or move to eldercare facilities, another round of young couples wouldn't be moving in. Instead, real estate developers have been tearing the old houses down and building monstrous new houses on spec, cashing out in a metropolitan area growing by a hundred people a day.

My old neighborhood isn't recognizable anymore, and neither is much of this city, my home for more than thirty years. There are many reasons to celebrate growth, and I don't want to be like the cranky old neighbor who stood in front of our house and complained that we were driving up his property taxes without acknowledging that we were also driving up his property's value. It's nothing less than a luxury to live in neighborhood like this. Most people in the world would love to live in a place where the biggest problem is that the new houses are so big the old trees keep dying, their roots covered in concrete and cinder block.

But something crucial is lost, too, when a city becomes a place where many of the people who work there can't even afford to live in the same county. No matter how much you love your neighbors, something important is lost when a community becomes a place where only the well-off can afford to live—where a single parent will never again buy a house, where schoolteachers with a baby on the way will never again buy a house, where there's no little rental house perfect for a lonely widow to move into, right across the street from her daughter.

THE GIFT OF SHARED GRIEF

It's hard to know what to say to people in mourning.
Say something anyway.

FEBRUARY 4, 2019

When my mother died in 2012, she left behind a huge collection of memorabilia. Not just the usual love letters, family photographs, and cherished recipe cards but also random items that almost no one else bothers to save. Parking tickets. Embossed cocktail napkins from the weddings of people I'd never heard of. An Alabama Power bill from 1972. Things that meant something to her but whose meaning she never explained to me.

Among those chance pieces of paper, I found my own 1980 report card from our church's Sunday school program. My teacher was Leo M. Hall, the father of two of my closest friends. Dr. Hall was a decorated medical school professor of biochemistry and molecular genetics at the University of Alabama at Birmingham, but he also taught a high school religion class every Sunday afternoon during my teenage years. It was an unpaid act of service that I'm sure I didn't recognize at the time for the true gift it was. How many religion students are taught by a scientist? How many high schoolers are taught by a college professor who is untroubled by skepticism or dissent? How many white Southerners of my generation grew up with a mentor who was a passionate advocate for civil rights?

I saved the report card, just as my mother had, and probably for the same reason: the teacher's comments at the bottom of the page. In his final remarks of the school year, Dr. Hall had written: "Stimulates conversation—likes the controversial topic, accepts a challenge readily. Can be a bit abrasive with classmates but has improved greatly during the last three years. Deep spiritual life. Widely read. A delightful young woman who will do well in her mature days."

I am well into my mature days now, and I don't much remember the eighteen-year-old girl Dr. Hall is describing, but I believe this to have been a fair assessment of my strengths and weaknesses at the time. ("Delightful" was, and still is, a stretch.)

When Dr. Hall died this past fall, I wasn't able to drive to Birmingham for his funeral because my husband had just had surgery, so I pulled that report card out of my mother's things and read it again, trying to find the right words to write in a letter to his widow. I remembered the good man who had meant so much to me at such an important time in my life. Someone who saw me clearly as I was and who looked past my faults to the possibilities of goodness. Someone who believed in the person I could yet become, long after I had left his religion class behind.

It's not easy to put into words what such a person means, and I have not always been the most faithful correspondent where condolence letters are concerned. But I have lost most of the beloved adults in my family now, and I know what a gift a few words of shared sadness can be.

When my mother died, I saved every card, every letter, every enclosure that came with every flower arrangement or potted plant. I printed out every email. I even copied all the Facebook messages into a document and printed that out, too. I was desperate to hold on to any shred of evidence that her life mattered, and to far more people than just my brother and sister and me. I needed to keep learning about her from others, now that she was no longer there to keep revealing herself in real time. I needed to be reminded that my own memories were not the only ones keeping her in the world.

On the worst days in the months that followed, I pulled out those reminders and read them again and again and again. Oftentimes I could swear I'd never read them before, though I knew I'd already read them all, and more than once. The shock of grief made me lose track of all manner of kindnesses in those first impossible days. I completely forgot that five of my neighborhood friends had driven all the way to Birmingham for the funeral. I had hugged them, I had cried on their shoulders, and then I had forgotten they had come. Their notes of love and remembrance, when I pulled them out later, helped me remember again, too.

A condolence letter is a gift to the recipient, but it's a gift to the writer, too. Remembering someone you loved is a way of remembering who you were, a way of linking your own past and present. Even when you love only the survivor—even if you hardly knew, or never met, the mourned beloved—you know something crucial: you know that person had a hand in creating someone you love. A condolence letter confirms the necessity of connection, one human heart to another. It's a way of saying, "We belong to one another." Or, as John Donne put it far more beautifully, "Any man's death diminishes me, because I am involved in mankind."

We live in a culture that celebrates youth and vitality far more than it prizes age and experience. Much as we might prefer to avert our eyes from the inevitable, we are mortal beings, and there is no escaping death, others' or our own. Writing a condolence letter is an act of shared humanity. It needn't be perfect, and it needn't be a tome. It's enough to say: "I'm so sorry. I know how much you loved her. I miss her, too."

REMEMBRANCE OF
RECIPES PAST

Thanksgiving is the one time of year when family bonds
matter more than the food.

NOVEMBER 19, 2018

All fall, in random hours, I've been looking for my great-grandmother's recipe for corn cakes. I have a perfectly serviceable recipe for everyday cornbread, but it's nothing like those corn cakes I find myself returning to in memory. My cornbread is prepared in the usual way and baked as cornbread should always be baked: in a cast-iron skillet. I've made it so many times I don't need to consult the recipe anymore, and maybe that's the reason I've never found the recipe for my great-grandmother's corn cakes, too. It's likely there never was a recipe.

I keep searching because winter makes me long for those glistening golden discs that Mother Ollie made right on the stovetop, dropping a dollop of thin batter, pancake style, into a shallow pool of heated oil in her own cast-iron skillet. The circles would spread out in the oil, thinner and thinner, until a kind of lace formed around the edges. A proper corn cake is golden in the center, soft and puffy, with lacy edges that are crisp and almost brown.

Mother Ollie's cooking technique I remember well enough; it's her recipe for the batter that's lost to me now. I found her recipe for gruel ("good for ailing folks," the card notes) and a recipe in my grandmother's hand for buttermilk

213

rolls, as well as two different copies of the cream cheese pound cake invented by Miss Tommie, my grandmother's best friend. But in the recipe box I inherited from my mother there is no card for corn cakes.

The internet is full of recipes for every possible kind of cornbread. Google "lacy corn cakes," and half a dozen recipes will pop up, though none of them look just right in the pictures. Some call for a mixture of plain cornmeal and flour; some call for self-rising cornmeal; some require buttermilk, and some make do with water. It's a surprising variety of options for a food rarely made from more than four ingredients, and I tell myself I don't have time to test them all.

The truth is that I don't want to cook from a stranger's recipe. I want to cook from a family recipe. It's Thanksgiving, when I am always homesick. I am searching for a particular taste, for a mixture of corn and salt and butter that will take me instantly back to a farmhouse in Lower Alabama, the house where my people lived for generations. I want my kitchen to be filled with the same scents that came from that old kitchen when the house was full of family.

The recipe I'm looking for might still turn up. In her life, my mother created inscrutable taxonomies of every kind, and the cards in her recipe box were no exception. Just because a cornbread recipe isn't in the bread section does not mean it isn't in the box somewhere else. And there are hundreds of recipe cards that aren't in the box at all anymore because Mom pulled them out and never put them back.

During the last years of her life, she ate supper at my house every night. Her own stove was unplugged for safety's sake, and there was no reason for her to spend hours poring over recipes for dishes she was never going to cook. She left the cards in little piles all over her house even so—on bookcase shelves, on the floor beside her bed, on every side table in every room. In the days after she died, I gathered them up and dumped them into various baskets and boxes. I still can't bring myself to sort through them.

When I was growing up, my mother put a hot meal on the table every night, but she was never an enthusiastic cook—no one greeted the invention of Hamburger Helper with more gratitude. I don't know why, decades later, she kept pulling out the recipe cards. Maybe she was looking for a particular recipe, too, hoping I might be persuaded to cook a dish she remembered and suddenly missed. Or maybe she wanted only to remember her own beloved dead.

For me it is always both heartbreaking and comforting to open my mother's recipe box on a rainy Sunday afternoon. The family Thanksgiving recipes are there, of course—the squash dressing, creamed spinach, and pecan pie that my children regard as holiday nonnegotiables in the same way I did when I was in my twenties and feeling both the intoxication and anxiety of independence. Thanksgiving is not a time for culinary experimentation, at least not in our family. There's comfort in a traditional holiday meal that goes far beyond the notion of comfort food.

But my mother's recipe box is also a kind of living document, an annotated interplay of generations. Recipes in my great-grandmother's hand are adjusted in my grandmother's, and then again in my mother's. Tucked behind Mom's recipe for a ground-beef-and-sour-cream casserole is my recipe for spinach lasagna—I don't remember copying it out for Mom, but I recognize the notebook paper I habitually used in graduate school. There's a recipe for pork tenderloin in my mother-in-law's handwriting, too, and countless recipes from friends and relations whose handwriting I can still identify even decades after their deaths. I could create a timeline of my own life from those recipe cards.

My children have grown up eating Sister Shubert's rolls on Thanksgiving Day, and they will not be brokenhearted if I never find Mother Ollie's recipe for corn cakes, though I am not giving up the search. Even if I don't find it in time, I hope my grandmother's recipe for yeast rolls, newly recovered from the unfathomable mysteries of my mother's recipe box, will fill my kitchen with the scent of home. Perhaps the secret is in the buttermilk.

ALL THE EMPTY SEATS AT
THE TABLE

*Even before the pandemic, Thanksgiving was a
reminder of loved ones gone before.*

NOVEMBER 23, 2020

In the box of old photos I found after my mother's death, there's a picture of me taken on Thanksgiving Day 1983, in the fall of my senior year of college. I'm lying on the sofa reading James Agee's letters to Father Flye. I don't know why the photo exists—we were not a family who documented ordinary moments. Our pictures centered on people gathered around birthday cakes and Christmas trees. Film wasn't wasted on someone who has no idea a picture is being taken. Certainly not on someone who isn't even smiling.

I remember that day not because it was documented in a photograph but because I ran into my Shakespeare professor outside the liberal arts building when I got back to school, and he asked me how I'd spent the break. "All I did was eat and sleep and read James Agee," I told him. "That sounds like the perfect Thanksgiving," he said.

Maybe I remember that conversation because it startled me. It had not felt like the perfect Thanksgiving. My great-grandmother, the quiet, steady, patient anchor of the entire extended family, was missing. She'd broken her hip the year before, at age ninety-six, and then pneumonia—"the old folks' friend," my great-grandfather, a country doctor, called it—had taken hold. Mother Ollie was still herself right until up until the day she fell, and I suppose that's what my great-grandfather must have meant by "friend": that there are fates worse than death for the very aged. But a year later, the empty place at the table still felt like a rebuke. As with every death before or since, I could not get over the shock. How can love not be enough to save someone so deeply loved?

A year earlier, too, my grandmother had barely survived a shooting that shattered the feeling of safety in her close-knit farming community. She recovered, eventually, but she always needed help after that, and holidays shifted to our house. All the Thanksgiving gatherings of my childhood, the sideboards laid with pies and casseroles and corn cakes glistening with butter, with bowls of creamed corn and lady peas; the arrangements of pink camellias and the delicate custard dishes of ambrosia, each with a sprinkling of coconut on top; the rocking on the porch afterward, the catching-up talk and the stories about loved ones long since buried in the graveyard just down the road—all of it was gone.

One year my grandmother was still cooking the feast she had always prepared, and the next year it was just our family at our own ordinary house in the ordinary suburbs. Overnight, it seemed, my mother became the de facto matriarch, and it was not a role she ever came to relish.

Mom would have been happy to serve stuffing out of a box and cranberry sauce out of a can, but my father was committed to the traditions he had acquired by marriage. A child of the Depression, growing up with a single mother forced to travel for work, he spent most of his childhood in what amounted to an orphanage. Having gained an extended family at the age of thirty-two, he would not give up the groaning table so easily and thereafter pitched in as a wholehearted sous chef. Mother Ollie took the recipe for corn cakes with her to the grave, but the scaled-back Thanksgiving menu at our house included almost all the other favorites—plus, it must be said, some horrific innovations, like brandied fruit and cranberry Jell-O mold, that my mother must have picked up from a magazine.

After I left home, I came to recognize the gift of those gatherings, of being with my family together under one roof, but Thanksgiving never stopped reminding me of that homely old house in the country with pecan trees to climb and cousins to play with and bird dogs sleeping in a patch of sunshine in the yard. Of all the empty seats at the table.

Now I am the matriarch, the one who cuts the flowers and puts them in vases, the one who spends days in the kitchen, chopping and sautéing and stirring and buttering, all for the sake of two hours at the table with everyone we love. My own husband is the wholehearted sous chef these days, but I admit that there have been times when I was still cross about it all. Times when, like my mother, I didn't want to be the matriarch. Why hadn't I understood, all those years before, what luck it was to be the cherished child returning home, with a whole day set aside for eating and sleeping and reading the intoxicating words of James Agee?

But today I am wondering why I haven't always appreciated the crowded house and the days of preparation for the two-table feasts of my own matriarch years. In this pandemic holiday, no one will gather here but our adult children, and once again there will be too many empty seats at the table. That's a metaphor: in fact there will be no table, for we'll be sitting outside with our plates in our laps, trusting the distance and the open air to keep us safe.

If my sons ever look back at photos of this gathering from the vantage of decades, they will surely see a poor approximation of their own Thanksgivings past: no aunts and uncles this year, no cousins, no beloved friends. The pictures won't remind them that when it came time for the blessing, we gave thanks that our bouts with the virus have all been relatively mild, or that we prayed for the families, more than a quarter of a million already, who will have empty chairs at their own tables forever after. That we prayed for our country as winter came on.

But maybe they will remember the joy of being together for a little while, if only at a distance, and the quiet pleasure of an unencumbered afternoon at the end of a hard, hard year. I hope they will know somehow, even if no one thinks to tell them, that such days are rare—and truly perfect.

WHAT IT MEANS TO BE
#NASHVILLESTRONG

*The tornadoes that tore through Middle Tennessee felt
like the apocalypse. But people here had other plans.*

MARCH 8, 2020

My husband and I would have slept through the tornado that hit Nashville in the middle of the night last week, but our nocturnal middle son woke us up to say his phone had just issued a tornado warning. In our neighborhood, the wind was hardly blowing.

True, it was unseasonably warm for early March. And in winter, warm temperatures often herald storms. But earlier in the evening the National Weather Service had calculated the likelihood of severe weather during the night as "a slight risk," with a 2 percent chance of tornadoes within twenty-five miles of Nashville. We got up just in case.

My husband turned on a local news channel. I opened Twitter and pulled up the Nashville Severe Weather account, my go-to source for up-to-the-minute information on changing weather in the area. Here is the first tweet I saw: "Confirmed tornado northwest of Downtown Nashville. TAKE COVER NOW IF YOU ARE IN DAVIDSON, WILSON, OR SUMNER COUNTIES!" Shortly after that, Sam Shamburger, lead forecaster for the National Weather Service in Nashville, tweeted a video of the tornado moving through downtown, just north of the Tennessee State Capitol.

I watched that video over and over again, trying to understand what I was seeing with my own eyes and yet not seeing at all: six miles away, people were being thrown from their beds, thrown from their homes. Windows were exploding, walls were collapsing, roofs were carried away into the sky, enormous trees were being wrenched from the ground. None of it was touching me. Barely a leaf stirred in my yard. How was it possible for something so monstrous and so nearby to be, at the same time, so utterly invisible?

By first light, the scope of the tragedy was already becoming clear: whole swaths of the city—neighborhoods and schools and businesses and churches—ground into rubble. Twenty-five people across the region, almost all of them in the Cookeville area, where the monster twister reached a magnitude of EF-4, were killed in their sleep. Among the dead were young and old, well-off and poor.

It's pointless to rank suffering. Loss is always loss. Grief is always grief. Tornadoes aren't worse than hurricanes or flash floods or wildfires. But tornadoes are unique among natural disasters in the pure randomness of their destruction. They can slam one house to splinters and leave teacups untouched on the kitchen table next door. They can hopscotch around a city, reaching down here and there, unpredictably, like a malevolent finger rubbing out an ant. It's the arbitrariness of the destruction, as much as its shocking power, that makes a tornado so fearsome. We don't deserve the suffering it brings. We cannot protect ourselves against it.

Photos and drone videos of the tornadoes' aftermath reveal exactly what you expect them to reveal. People picking through piles of debris, people embracing, people bowing their heads in prayer. Row after row of apartments and cottages, their facades peeled away as in a shadow box, opening to full view the private lives that unfolded within. The floral sheets. The brass chandeliers. The Formica countertops. It's impossible not to feel a tenderness for the lives of those strangers, an urge to tiptoe up and pull the door closed, to unsee what we were never meant to see, to give them back their secrets.

Perhaps that's why Nashville has responded to the wreckage by urgently pitching in. All across this city, people are showing up to help friends and strangers. They are showing up with work gloves and chain saws and garbage bags and tarps. They are making casseroles by the dozens and sandwiches by the hundreds. They are making repeat trips to big-box stores for flashlights and batteries and blankets and nonperishable food and baby formula and diapers and tampons and hand wipes and over-the-counter medicines, and then they are giving it all away.

Some of this is happening through the expert efforts of existing community organizations like Hands On Nashville, Gideon's Army, the Second Harvest Food Bank of Middle Tennessee, and the Community Resource Center Nashville. Some of it is happening organically, as people hear from somebody who knows somebody who needs help. Some of it is happening because people keep showing up and looking around for an opportunity to help—so, so many people that it can sometimes become a problem for power crews with heavy equipment trying to get through.

And what would Music City be without a benefit concert or ten? Or a plan to help get musicians themselves back on their feet? People who can't help in person are donating to the Middle Tennessee Emergency Response Fund or GoFundMe campaigns that now routinely top their target goals. All by herself, Taylor Swift gave $1 million to tornado relief.

None of this is surprising. This is what Southerners are famous for. The response to Middle Tennessee's tornadoes is simply a barn raising in the city, the death-in-the-family casserole and the Sunday second collection writ large. Like all emotional states, compassion is infectious.

The day after the tornadoes, I was texting with a friend who moved to Middle Tennessee from Bay St. Louis, Mississippi. Her family had made it through Hurricane Katrina, a calamity that happened on a far larger scale, but making comparisons wasn't what was on her mind. "Louis and I now talk about the 'private Katrina' our friends might have: cancer, death of a child, you name it. One day the sun is shining and all is intact, the next day everything is broken. And the rest of the world goes on. You're trapped in your own crazy snow globe that's been shaken so hard all the pieces fly loose."

This is a truth we all instinctively recognize. That random funnel cloud of death and destruction could have happened anywhere—it could come for any of us at any time. And while we understand that we have not been singled out by God for survival, we also understand that we can be God's hands here in the rubble, helping our neighbors dig out.

THE NIGHT THE LIGHTS
WENT OUT

*This year has brought tornadoes, plague, and weather
patterns we've never heard of. On the bright side,
no murder hornets yet.*

MAY 11, 2020

By March 22, the day Mayor John Cooper issued a safer-at-home order here to slow the transmission of the coronavirus, our city had already been in crisis mode for nearly three weeks. Monster tornadoes had ripped through this region, killing twenty-five people and demolishing hundreds of buildings, including nearly four hundred homes in Nashville alone. And it's pretty hard to shelter in place when your shelter has just taken a ride through the sky.

The storms that hit last week were milder by comparison, but Tennesseans still began to mutter darkly about divine retribution. "Tornadoes, Covid, no power," tweeted the musician Kendell Marvel, taking a shot at big-hat country radio, "it's almost like Nashville is being punished for all the years of mediocre music."

Part of the dismay stems from the unusual weather itself. A rare system called a derecho sent hurricane-force straight-line winds blowing across Middle Tennessee, toppling ancient trees and power poles and leaving 131,000 people without electricity. Heroic Nashville Electric Service crews—which, because of concerns about the coronavirus, were working through the night without the usual assistance

225

from teams in nearby states—got that number down to about 80,000 on Monday. That was before a weather system called a wake low, also rare, triggered yet another round of powerful storms and brought the number of people without power back up to 120,000.

Coming on the heels of a deadly virus that has never been seen in humans before, the unusual storms introduced a reasonable question: Why does the natural world keep finding new ways to kill us?

On the bright side, no sign of murder hornets here yet.

Losing power on Sunday night is one thing, but lacking power on a workday feels almost calamitous, especially when libraries and coffee shops, the satellite "offices" that telecommuters rely on, are already closed. When the electric utility announced that outages were so extensive as to be unprecedented and that getting everyone back on the grid could take one to two weeks, there was a great groaning in Nashville.

I was not entirely troubled by this turn of events, I have to admit. I missed the hot showers—oh, how I missed the hot showers!—but the four broken power poles that spilled live wires onto my street meant lighter traffic in the neighborhood, and the lack of power itself provided a good excuse to let unanswered emails languish. I loved hearing our youngest boys, home now because the pandemic has filled this empty nest back up, laughing with each other over a game of cards instead of being hunched over their personal screens.

I figured a week of spit baths would be a good trade for nights around the kitchen table, all of us reading together by candlelight. Not everyone in my family feels this way, but for me those nights were a pure pleasure made perfect by the book at hand: *This Is Happiness* by the Irish novelist Niall Williams, about the coming of electricity to a remote village, a book so beautiful and so funny and so true that it will make you love the whole human race and forgive it all its trespasses.

Plus, this has been the loveliest spring imaginable, cool and damp and green, the old-timey kind of Middle Tennessee springtime that we used to get every year and now get almost never, a gentle, rainy springtime that keeps the flowers blooming for days and days and fills the trees with birdsong. Opening the windows to a spring like this one, at a time when the neighborhood machinery has fallen silent and the crickets and the screech owls are the only sounds in the air, is nothing less than a gift.

To take a walk at night in a city that has settled into silence and a darkness that has become far too rare is to return to something precious, something lost for so long you've forgotten to miss it. When it comes back to you unbidden, when that big pie plate of a moon and that star-drenched sky bless you as you walk down the middle of your street, right down the middle of the street, with your head thrown back and your mouth fallen open, that's something more than a gift. It's a walk through the past, a walk in the present, and possibly—if we can't change our lives in time to head off the coming environmental collapse—a walk into the future. All at once.

It's a time of neighborliness, as everyone looks in on the elderly and the lonely, checking to be sure they're making do and guessing together about when the lights might come back on. A time when people stand in the street and linger, talking. For what is there to rush back to at the silent houses? A time when children play outside long past dark and go to bed dirty, their hair still smelling of that old sweet scent of childhood: sunlight and soil and sweat.

Walking the dark street, you can see the candles lighting one room of a neighbor's house and then move, disembodied, into the next, finally going dark as you move toward home yourself. As you strike a match to send a light into the darkness from your own window, too.

But then, only three days into the power outage, the heroes of the Nashville Electric Service arrived to perform their magnificent magic, stringing lines and erecting monster poles and hauling themselves up and down, up and down, sometimes with bucket trucks but sometimes with nothing but their own good muscles, a tool belt, and some spiked shoes, for fifteen hours straight.

When, finally, the lights came on, all the people standing in the street erupted into cheers and thank-yous—but not hugs and handshakes, for there's still a pandemic to fear— and walked on home, laughing under streetlights, and stars they could no longer see.

THE STORY OF THE SURLY SANTA AND THE CHRISTMAS MIRACLE

The smallest gifts can be the ones
that linger longest in memory.

DECEMBER 23, 2019

It was 1994, a week before Christmas, when my not-quite-three-year-old spied a shopping mall Santa and insisted on paying him another visit. I tried to demur. I tried to deflect. His official Santa visit had taken place weeks earlier. This trip to the mall was just a chance to escape the gloom that is Nashville in December, to wear out those busy toddler legs in a place where it wasn't raining and cold. We planned to ride a few escalators and throw a few pennies into the fountain: "I wish for a brudder!" my child yelled with every splash of a copper coin, and all the nearby shoppers smiled. I could not smile.

Then the not-quite-three-year-old caught sight of Santa, that mythical person of endless bounty. Here was a chance to see the great man one more time before he came secretly and invisibly to our own house in the dark of night!

Santa himself was less enthusiastic. Perhaps "surly" is just the default position of a shopping mall Santa in the week before Christmas. When my boy held his arms up for a boost onto the big man's lap, Santa simply looked at me. Finally I did the hoisting myself. "Ho, ho, ho," Santa said. There was no exclamation point after the last "ho."

My son smiled beatifically, confident of Santa's love and largesse. "I yike a golden trumpet!" he announced.

Behind him, I gave a tight-lipped shake of my head. Santa did not meet my eyes.

"I yike a pitchfork!" my child continued. "A real pitchfork."

Now I was sending desperate semaphores toward the man with the bag. "Please, no," my eyes begged. "Please tell him he can't have a pitchfork for Christmas." Santa ignored me.

"Have you been a good boy this year?" he asked. Yes, yes, my son nodded. "Then of course you can have a golden trumpet," Santa said. "Of course you can have a pitchfork for Christmas." He looked at me. The expression on his face, even all these years later, is hard to describe. It looked for all the world like revenge.

I should've seen the whole thing coming. A year earlier, two days before Christmas, a black-and-orange moving van had pulled up in front of our house and the next-door neighbors' house, too—a truck so large it spanned the street side of both lots. My boy stood on our sofa for most of that day, watching through the window as workers loaded all our neighbors' worldly belongings onto that unfathomably large vehicle. At dusk, when they were done, the truck began to back up, beeping all the way. My son hopped up and down, clapping his hands in glee. Then he revised his Christmas list: it suddenly consisted solely of a black-and-orange truck that beeped in reverse. By the grace of God and Toys "R" Us, Santa found one.

But a golden trumpet? A pitchfork? I was pretty sure pitchforks were not part of the Toys "R" Us inventory. This time Santa was going to need serious backup.

Four grandparents, a great-aunt, a great-great-aunt, and

all seven sets of regular aunts and uncles were dispatched on a search that spanned five states. For days the phone rang with reports. An ornamental French horn had been located in a florist-supply shop: it didn't make noise, but it was golden, and it would fit a child's hands. A miniature rake had turned up in a gardening catalog, and maybe a rake was close enough to a pitchfork? Would a real pennywhistle work in lieu of a trumpet?

In the end, a toy trumpet made of white plastic arrived via two-day mail, along with a decorative French horn—golden but silent—for good measure. On Christmas morning, a handsome child-size rake stood in for the pitchfork beneath the tree. The delighted child in red footie pajamas didn't seem to notice the substitution.

All this sounds hopelessly indulgent, I know, a rookie mistake by parents—and an entire extended family—who hadn't yet figured out that they aren't doing their children any favors when they protect them from every possible disappointment.

But that year our house was permeated by sadness, and I didn't see how I could bear any more of it. The boy who shouted, "I wish for a brudder!" every time he threw a penny into a shopping mall fountain could not have known that his mother had just suffered a miscarriage. He didn't understand what it meant that tears sprang to her eyes with every wish he made at that fountain. He didn't understand his father's feeling of helplessness.

So we might not be able to give him a brother, but by God we would find him a trumpet. And the entire extended family, on both sides, was determined to help. Together, we would find that child something that passed for a pitchfork, even if it meant paying too much for mail-order garden equipment.

That was twenty-five years ago, and the not-quite-three-year-old is now a man. All but one of his grandparents are gone, and both great-aunts, too. Even the shopping mall is gone. But not everything is gone.

I didn't know it in 1994, but my firstborn would eventually get his wish for not one brother but two. The aunts and uncles who loved him then still love him now, and next summer they will gather for his wedding. They will stand behind him as he begins a new life and a new family, a reminder that the new little family is not alone in the world. Their loved ones will be there to see them through whatever comes their way.

Every year I find myself thinking of that Christmas, when a surly Santa gave our entire clan a chance to surround our family with love—the chance, collectively, to keep the magic alive for one little boy with a sad mother and a bewildered father who didn't know how to help the sadness. It was not the happiest Christmas of my life, and it was not the grandest, but it is the one I won't ever forget.

TRUE LOVE IN THE AGE OF CORONAVIRUS

*The pandemic turned our plans upside down, but in
the end the day was perfect.*

JULY 27, 2020

When our oldest son got engaged last year at sunset on a beach in Spain, my husband and I cheered from half a world away. The parents of three sons, we would have a daughter at last, and we already loved this amazing young woman. We loved how happy she and our son make each other. We loved the way they support and challenge and admire each other, the way they are always laughing together. They are the kind of people who would rather save up for a grand backpacking adventure than a grand engagement ring, and we loved how a ring made from my great-grandmother's tiny diamond made its way to Spain in a special wooden box that my son carried in his pocket, waiting for just the right moment to drop to one knee.

It was always going to be a small, do-it-yourself event: just family and their dearest friends at Cedars of Lebanon State Park, in a historic lodge that seats only seventy-five people. A newly minted college graduate would be the photographer. A fellow nurse at the hospital where my daughter-in-law works would bake the cake. I would grow the wedding flowers, and the bride's mother would make the tablecloths for the reception. But no matter how simple it looks or how homey it feels, a DIY wedding requires a lot of planning.

The coronavirus turned all those plans upside down, requiring new plans, and then newer plans, as the pandemic worsened, with wildfire infections spreading across cities and rural counties alike. Twelve days before the wedding, Governor Bill Lee extended Tennessee's state of emergency for another two months.

The bride's mother started making masks—enough for every single guest and member of the wedding party. The half-hour ceremony got streamlined to fifteen minutes. Plans for the reception shifted to an outdoor patio, never mind that afternoon temperatures in July average ninety degrees in Middle Tennessee. Bottles of hand sanitizer would be nestled among the flower arrangements at every table.

Even so, the guests were getting nervous. Family members of my generation began to send regrets. New York added Tennessee to the list of states from which visitors would be forced to quarantine after entering. One of my son's groomsmen, a childhood friend who now lives in New York City, decided he couldn't afford to lose those two weeks and sent his regrets, too.

As their wedding day approached, the happy couple was becoming a worried couple. Tennessee's state of emergency limits social gatherings to fifty people or fewer, although that requirement does not apply to funerals, weddings, or church services. Legally, then, the wedding could go on as planned, and those plans now included every safety measure any of us could think of. But there is more to a pandemic wedding than questions of legality, and clearly the tenor of this event had already changed. Was it truly safe? Would guests spend the whole time uneasy and subdued?

With eight days to go, my son and daughter-in-law sent an email to their entire guest list that effectively canceled the wedding. The ceremony would still take place; there just wouldn't be any guests in Cedar Forest Lodge to witness it. "We both love each and every one of you and it truly breaks our hearts to make this decision, but we both know that the best decision isn't always the easiest to make," my son wrote. "We also know that a wedding is just one day in our lives and a wedding doesn't make a marriage."

They are not alone. Just among our closest friends, one wedding has been postponed indefinitely and another finally took place, two months late, in the bride's sister's backyard. Here in the United States, the $74 billion wedding industry has come to a grinding halt. Abroad, it took three tries for Prime Minister Mette Frederiksen of Denmark to find a wedding date that would stick, and the rescheduled wedding for Princess Beatrice of Britain included only immediate family.

In the end, our own family's pandemic wedding was absolutely perfect. Parents and siblings joined the couple in the hall; grandparents, aunts and uncles, cousins and friends watched via Zoom. When the time came to make their vows, to promise that they would love each other through good times and bad, in sickness and in health, our son and daughter-in-law stood in front of a window installed during the Great Depression by workers who knew something about unearned suffering.

They stood and gazed at each other in front of that sun-drenched window, and I think they surely had no sense at all of how many loved ones were missing from the echoing hall. They didn't know because his eyes never left hers, and because her eyes never left his, and because the promises they made, however publicly such vows are spoken in a wedding ceremony, are promises that belong to the two of them alone.

ARTS
& CULTURE

KEEP AMERICA'S
ROADSIDE WEIRD

We brake for giant chickens. And peaches. And Vulcans.
You probably should, too.

AUGUST 25, 2018

M y husband and I were driving down I-65, still in
Tennessee but near the Alabama border, when
the statue of a giant chicken caught my eye. It was
standing in front of a truck stop near Elkton. I am grateful to
be married to a man who will instantly pull off the highway
when someone says, "Hey, let's take a selfie with that chicken!"

That particular chicken is an advertisement for the Shady
Lawn Truck Stop's fried-chicken plate. It is wearing a chef's
hat. Tucked under its wings are a giant fork and a giant
carving knife. The combination makes for a troubling message: chicken as both dinner and diner. It is also covered
with graffiti, mostly people's names but also an exhortation
to "Read More." Unlike the existential conflict at the heart
of the chicken's identity, that's a message I had no trouble
decoding.

Between Nashville and the Alabama Gulf Coast,
where my husband and I were heading, there are quite a
few unusual roadside attractions. An actual Saturn rocket,
all 224 feet of it, is posed as if for blastoff at the Alabama
welcome center near Ardmore. The Ave Maria Grotto,
where a Benedictine monk built 125 miniature replicas of
famous religious sites—all made in part from found objects

like cold-cream jars and toilet floaters—occupies a four-acre park in Cullman.

In Birmingham, fifty miles south of this "Jerusalem in miniature," the cosmology goes back even further. Rising above the city is a mammoth statue of Vulcan, the Roman god of the forge. It is the world's largest cast-iron statue, but during the years when I was growing up there, its fame lay primarily in its peculiar attire: Vulcan is wearing nothing but a blacksmith's apron and knee-high sandals, and his bare buttocks moon the town of Homewood.

Perhaps because that image is still fresh in mind by the time drivers on I-65 reach the water tower in Chilton County, center of the Alabama peach-growing region, it's hard not to see a connection between Birmingham's famous landmark and Chilton County's almost-as-famous water tower, which was built in the shape of an authentically cleft peach. (Ask yourself what anatomical feature a peach most resembles.)

Barely ten miles down the road, as if to punish such thoughts, there's a billboard directing motorists to "GO TO CHURCH Or the Devil Will Get You!" This billboard graced the interstate near Prattville for many decades before a storm knocked it down in 2016. Last year heavy rains kept the surrounding soil too wet for the necessary repairs. "The devil is trying to knock it all down, but we're going to get it back up," the son of the Montgomery man who first erected the billboard told a reporter. Satan apparently lost the battle this year, and the sign is back in place, the original red-tailed devil intact. And the monstrous red scythe the devil is holding could surely take even the Elkton chicken's carving knife in a fight.

Nearby Montgomery boasts the World's Largest Brick Made of Bricks. (Once the World's Largest Brick period, it was bested in 2007 by a slightly larger brick built in one piece.) We didn't stop to see it, but we did stop for five more giant chickens—some metal, some concrete—that were standing in front of various small-town establishments off the interstate.

These are some of the roadside highlights along one stretch of one highway, mind you. The peach-shaped water tower in Chilton County is half the size of the Peachoid in Gaffney, South Carolina. The giant chicken outside Elkton has nothing on the World's Largest Prairie Dog in Cactus Flat, South Dakota. I know because we stopped to see the prairie dog in 2006. We also stopped in Collinsville, Illinois, to see the World's Largest Catsup Bottle. Both stops occurred on the way to Mt. Rushmore, which my husband still calls "The World's Largest Carving of Presidential Heads."

All across the country, on interstates the width of football fields and two-lane blue highways, stand an uncountable number of homespun reminders that American ingenuity and wit have not yet been Walmart-ized out of existence. Think of Carhenge in Alliance, Nebraska, a replica of Stonehenge made entirely of vintage automobiles. Think of Dog Bark Park Inn in Cottonwood, Idaho, a bed-and-breakfast that doubles as the World's Largest Beagle. Think of the thirteen-foot-tall peanut smiling with Jimmy Carter–style teeth in Plains, Georgia; or the World's Largest Ball of Twine in Cawker City, Kansas; or Lenny, the World's Only Life-Size Chocolate Moose, in Scarborough, Maine. Virtually every highway in the country is the site of at least one, especially here in the South.

They are most visible on leisurely summer road trips, when a detour to take a selfie with a chicken or to snicker at a 114-year-old statue's bare butt won't make anyone late for the cranberry relish or the Easter ham, but they are always there.

Often meant to be an advertisement for some local enterprise, they are inevitably much more than the mercantile economy requires. They are also evidence that human imagination will always resist homogenization, that daring art isn't found only in galleries and museums, that wit and wile are everywhere among us. When interstate exits are marked by the instantly recognizable icons of a dozen fast-food restaurants and gas stations supplied by the same multinational oil companies, the giant roadside chickens will always remind us of who we are.

COUNTRY MUSIC AS
MELTING POT

*The new documentary series by Ken Burns aims to
remind divided Americans of what they have in common.*

SEPTEMBER 9, 2019

L ast spring at the Ryman Auditorium, sitting in the audience for a concert filmed to celebrate a new documentary series by Ken Burns, I couldn't help but notice that the folks around me didn't look much like the usual bro-country fans swarming Nashville these days. Just who exactly was this documentary aiming to reach?

All of us, it turns out. People of every age, every political persuasion, every socioeconomic class, every race. The goal of *Country Music* is nothing less than to remind us of who we really are. Even its cover image is designed to evoke the American flag.

Country music, Mr. Burns explained at the concert, is "a uniquely American art form," one whose signature instruments, the banjo and the fiddle, continue to transmit the disparate cultures, African and European, from which the music sprang. "Country music has never been one style of music," Mr. Burns said. "It has always been a mixture of many styles, springing from many roots and sprouting many new branches to create a complicated chorus of American voices joining together to tell a complicated American story."

For the sake of a television audience that might be unfamiliar with country music, all the famous stories are here.

How Hank Williams, "the Hillbilly Shakespeare," died in the back seat of a car during a snowstorm. How a young Willie Nelson drove to Patsy Cline's house in the middle of the night to play her the demo for "Crazy," a song he'd considered calling "Stupid." How Dolly Parton finally convinced Porter Wagoner to let her leave his television show by singing "I Will Always Love You," which she'd written for just that purpose. How Merle Haggard was an inmate in the audience during Johnny Cash's first concert at San Quentin prison. How Loretta Lynn, instructed not to hug Charley Pride onstage at the Country Music Awards, defied orders—hugging him and kissing him, too.

But it's the stories that aren't yet famous that will have faithful fans of the genre tuning in for every episode of *Country Music*. Mr. Burns's team listened to fifteen thousand songs; sifted through more than one hundred thousand photographs and six hundred hours of archival footage, much of it never before published; and conducted 101 on-camera interviews with country legends. The concert at the Ryman featured many of the stars who speak in the documentary.

Even so, it took a lot of courage to introduce this program at the mother church of country music. Half the people in this town are pickers, and the other half are music critics, professional or self-professed. But that hometown audience at the Ryman gasped out loud when a teenage Willie Nelson appeared in a photograph on the screen above the stage. *Country Music*, it turns out, could surprise even Music City.

One of the best decisions Mr. Burns made was to tell the story of country music primarily through its artists—those who knew the legends personally and now carry on their art—rather than through historians or critics. The result is a film that is both historically compelling and richly human. "Burns lifts these characters out of the history books and makes them rounded, imperfect humans," said Craig Havighurst, a Nashville music journalist and the author of *Air Castle of the South: WSM and the Making of Music City.* "The Carter Family's complexities and the tenacity and creative spirit of Mother Maybelle are made more vivid here than in any book I've read or documentary I've seen."

The singer-songwriter Vince Gill served as a consultant for the documentary, an experience that inspired him to call his own new album *Okie.* "After watching the *Country Music* film and learning about the origins of this music, from people of all backgrounds and races, I appreciated that Okies aren't that different from other groups who were scorned and stereotyped," he said. "They were hardworking people who were willing to do whatever it took to survive during one of our country's most challenging times. The people I grew up with were fair-minded and grounded by common sense. They have given me the values and traits I've carried with me on my life's journey, and they have inspired and created some of the best music I have ever heard."

Because country music is so strongly associated with white working-class people in the South, many of the same stereotypes that reduced impoverished farmers to "Okies" during the Dust Bowl years are still assigned to country music itself. But Mr. Burns takes pains to complicate these expectations, to highlight not just the story of an art form with roots in both slave quarters and mountain cabins but also the moral evolution of some of the genre's most prominent musicians.

Charley Pride's first recordings were released without biographical information. When fans finally found out that Mr. Pride is Black, many radio stations refused to play his singles.

"You son of a bitch, you go back there and tell that son of a bitch that manages your station if he takes Charley Pride off," Faron Young told one of them, "take all my records off." And it was country star Tom T. Hall who urged Johnny Rodriguez, the young Mexican American country singer whose manager billed him as Johnny Rogers, to come to Nashville and reclaim his name. The audience, he said, would come around.

More than anyone else, Johnny Cash pushed the country music establishment to embrace new artists and enfold new musical forms. Mr. Cash used the platform of his weekly network TV show to celebrate diversity and what his daughter Rosanne Cash calls the "ecumenical attitude he had toward all music." Guests included Stevie Wonder, Eric Clapton, the Who, James Taylor, Gordon Lightfoot, and Joni Mitchell. When network executives said Pete Seeger was too left-wing for the show, Mr. Cash ignored them. Mr. Seeger appeared anyway.

As Mr. Burns tells it, musical genres were always cross-pollinating. When Ringo Starr recorded a Buck Owens hit, "Act Naturally," the Beatles released it as the flip side of "Yesterday." Bob Dylan invited Johnny Cash to play the 1964 Newport Folk Festival and later moved his own recording work to Nashville; the success of *Blonde on Blonde* led a host of other folk and rock artists to Nashville studios, with Nashville session musicians sitting in. And as Willie Nelson observes about the diverse audiences who showed up for his annual Fourth of July concerts in Austin, college students and truck drivers aren't so different from each other after all: "They're out there drinking beer, smoking dope, and finding out that they really don't hate each other," he said.

Except for one ill-fated attempt to move away, I've lived in the South my whole life, and all my people are Southerners, but I didn't grow up listening to country music. My parents played only the big band tunes they'd danced to during their courtship, and the second I got my first transistor radio at age twelve, I tuned it to '70s rock. But as a homesick graduate student in Philadelphia, I found a country station on the radio and fell in love. It gave me what country music has been giving its listeners from the beginning: a way to feel less alone. That year I gave my parents Willie Nelson's *Stardust* for Christmas.

Every art form benefits from a gifted teacher, an expert, an evangelist—someone who can explain to the uninitiated or the skeptical or the heedless that, no, this actually isn't something their toddler could have made in nursery school. Someone who can convey the context in which the art was created, the hopes of its creators, the way they learned from each other and nudged each other to grow. Someone, above all, who can convince you that you will be better, your life more enriched, if you understand it.

Ken Burns, a Brooklyn-born filmmaker, may be an unlikely teacher of country music, but this comprehensive and nuanced documentary will make for a welcome reconsideration of the subject, especially for those who think they understand what country music is ("loving, cheating, hurting, fighting, drinking, pickup trucks, and Mother," as the late Harold Bradley described the stereotype) and those who think there's nothing much to understand. As Mr. Havighurst said, "I can't wait for America to see this and rethink what country music means and how it sounds."

JOHN PRINE:
AMERICAN ORACLE

*He wrote his first protest song in 1968, but this country
has never needed him more than it does now.*

Nine songs into his sold-out show at the Ryman
Auditorium here on October 5, John Prine stopped
singing long enough to give some context for a song
he wrote fifty years ago, during the height of the Vietnam War.
"I wrote this next one as a protest song," he said. "It was 1968,
and at the time we had a real jerk in the White House." He
paused before voicing what I was already thinking: "What a
coincidence."

Then he kicked off the famous anti-war anthem from his
1971 debut album, *John Prine*:

> *But your flag decal won't get you into Heaven anymore*
> *They're already overcrowded from your dirty little war*
> *Now Jesus don't like killin', no matter what the reason's for*
> *And your flag decal won't get you into Heaven anymore.*

In fact, that first record is full of protest songs, if you open
up the definition of "protest song" to include empathetic
ballads of lost souls, dreamers abandoned by the American
dream. "Sam Stone" first carried the much more pointed
title of "Great Society Conflict Veteran's Blues." With either
title, though, the song is an elegy, the story of an injured

soldier who leaves Vietnam with a morphine addiction, coming home "with a purple heart and a monkey on his back." "Angel from Montgomery" is a ballad in the voice of an old woman whose options have always been limited. "Hello in There" tells the story of two lonely elders who lost a son in Korea—"I still don't know what for, don't matter anymore."

Most haunting of all is "Paradise," a song named for the town in western Kentucky where Mr. Prine's parents were born. It tells of a rural childhood idyll that ends because:

> *The coal company came with the world's largest shovel*
> *And they tortured the timber and stripped all the land*
> *Well, they dug for their coal till the land was forsaken*
> *Then they wrote it all down as the progress of man.*

The damage is done, the song says; paradise has been razed, and there's nothing we can do about it now except to remember. But Mr. Prine's true story of Paradise, Kentucky, also spells out just what we have to lose in this gorgeous green world, and how permanent those losses are. Today, just as in 1971, the song reminds us of what happens when a gentle existence that lies easy on the land is destroyed for the profit of developers and corporations.

The difference between the way "Paradise" resonated with listeners in 1971 and the way we hear it now is that back then we didn't know what coal was doing to the planet itself. According to a new report from a United Nations panel of climate experts, the very industry that destroyed Paradise, Kentucky, is the one we must eliminate today or have no chance of curbing greenhouse gases in time to prevent global catastrophe. It also happens to be the industry Donald Trump vows to bring back. "We have ended the war on beautiful, clean coal," he said in this year's State of the Union address.

Mr. Prine's two-night residence at the Ryman was part of his tour for the release of *The Tree of Forgiveness*, the first record of original music he has made in thirteen years. This record, his twenty-fifth album, is classic John Prine: equally sweet and irreverent, written from a worldview where the heartbreaking and the ludicrous walk hand in hand.

No song on the new record is an overt protest song in the vein of "Sam Stone" or "Paradise," but the album's spare production echoes the powerful simplicity of Mr. Prine's first record, and the animating spirit of that early music is threaded throughout the new work, too. There are rollicking songs about knocking on a screen door in summertime or getting to heaven and smoking "a cigarette that's nine miles long," yes, but the one who's knocking on the screen door is a lonely drifter, and the one who's going to heaven is a songwriter who gave up smoking when he got throat cancer.

And tucked among these cheerful sad songs, too, are signs of the oracular John Prine, a prophet with his finger on the pulse of his times and his eyes turned always toward the world beyond. "The Lonesome Friends of Science" predicts the end of the world; "Caravan of Fools" links wealth with idiocy; the music video for "Summer's End" turns a haunting but elliptical song about randomness and failed dreams into a ballad for loved ones lost to the opioid epidemic. (The song is dedicated to Max Barry, the son of Nashville's former mayor, who died in the summer of 2017 of a drug overdose.)

From 1971 right through to today, John Prine has been a storyteller, not just between songs in a concert but within the songs themselves, and that's what gives them such power.

His primary mode of persuasion is the story, just as the primary mode of persuasion for the biblical Jesus is the parable. A parable has many advantages over a screed or a sermon (or, it must be said, an op-ed column). A parable trusts the story to do the work of conversion, and it trusts its listeners to do the work of interpretation. A parable resists polarities: people listening to a story can't immediately know whether they belong among the speaker's "us" or the speaker's "them."

The mother church of country music, where the seats are scratched-up pews and the windows are stained glass, is the place where the new John Prine—older now, scarred by cancer surgeries, his voice deeper and full of gravel—is most clearly still the old John Prine: mischievous, delighting in tomfoolery, but also worried about the world.

At the Ryman on October 5, the night when Mitch McConnell announced he had the votes to confirm Brett Kavanaugh for the Supreme Court, the songwriter who once called the United States on its dirty little war in Vietnam made an allusion to the controversy when he introduced "Angel from Montgomery." Dedicating the song to all the women in the audience, he said, "It's a sad, sad day when women can't be believed." This country has never needed John Prine more.

SO LONG TO MUSIC CITY'S
FAVORITE SOAP OPERA

*It's a wrap for the TV series, but the city
itself is still deciding what to be.*

APRIL 23, 2018

It was a Facebook video post by Charles Esten, who plays Deacon Claybourne on the TV series *Nashville*, that got me. Esten is sitting in a leather chair in the middle of the show's warehouse. The chair came from the set of Deacon's house, and Esten has just bought it as a memento of the six seasons he spent as a co-star on the show. "There's a million other things down here. If you're a fan of *Nashville*, you can own a piece of it," he says. "Come on down." So I did.

Nashville will begin airing its final eight episodes on June 7 on the Country Music Television channel. It began life on ABC in 2012 and was brought back from the dead, in true soap opera style, by CMT after ABC canceled it two years ago. If every single item on every single set—furniture, art, knickknacks, everything—was now for sale in a giant warehouse off Brick Church Pike, I realized, a second resurrection was clearly not at hand. But maybe I would find some sort of memento there, too.

The sale occupied two floors of the warehouse. I walked up to the door and stood still at the top of the ramp. "Holy cow," I said out loud. A woman nearby looked up and commented, "That's exactly what I said."

It wasn't just each character's favorite chair. It was hundreds and hundreds of chairs—armchairs, desk chairs, side chairs, church pews, barstools, and sofas. So many sofas. It wasn't just tables and lamps—it was spotlights, chandeliers, lighted mirrors, and bathroom sconces (plus the sinks, toilets, and urinals). There were bowls, vases, candles, and silk flowers. There were pool floaties in the shape of dragons, a life-size toy giraffe wearing a hat that said "Happy New Year," and, naturally, speakers, turntables, amps, guitars, and boxes and boxes of records.

I started watching *Nashville* because a friend of mine, a set decorator long exiled in Los Angeles, wanted to come home, and he wondered whether working for the show might be a way to get back. I started watching as a sign of solidarity, but I kept watching even after my friend decided to stay in LA.

I love old-school country—Loretta and Johnny and Waylon and Dolly—but I couldn't name a single one of the big-hat artists who fill stadiums and travel in giant caravans of eighteen-wheelers and tour buses, the kind of singer that *Nashville* is largely about.

The show offers exactly what you would expect of a nighttime soap opera: betrayal and bed hopping and addiction and murder and drunken confessions and gauzy-edged flashbacks and a surprising number of car crashes. The plotlines are ripe for ridicule, and Ashley Spurgeon's weekly recap of the show in the *Nashville Scene* is consistently one of the funniest things I read on the internet.

Nashville, like the real Nashville, has homeless people, but the homeless people in *Nashville* are invariably brilliant singers on a bad-luck streak. *Nashville*, like the real Nashville, is populated by celebrities, but the celebrities in *Nashville* are constantly being mobbed by paparazzi, even though there are no paparazzi here, and we pride ourselves on not pestering our celebrities. The show is like a Christmas-newsletter version of life in Music City: it's not entirely made up, but it's far enough from the truth for the people who live here to wonder how such an exactingly reproduced version of the city we live in could be so unlike the city we live in.

Still, I really do love this show and haven't missed a single episode. *Nashville* is worth an hour every week, if only for the songs. When it debuted, Emily Nussbaum wrote in *The New Yorker*, "For anyone who enjoys country music (if you have only nice things to say about the genre, come sit by me), the series has the added bonus of featuring live songs, sung in concert and in recording studios and occasionally at the Bluebird Cafe, a cozy (and real) joint where songwriters perform in the round."

"The real showstoppers on *Nashville*," wrote Jon Caramanica in *The Times*, are the "small songs, sung closely, in intimate rooms."

For me, one great attraction of *Nashville* is the way the imitation city in the television show highlights an identity crisis the real city is undergoing. We don't live in the perfectly designed sets of the city on TV, but we aren't the sleepy midsize city we used to be, either. We're the "it" city, in an area growing by roughly one hundred people a day, and we don't really know who we are anymore. When I see someone grabbing Keith and Nicole for a selfie at the movie theater, I have to bite my tongue to keep from saying, "Honey, we don't do that here." Apparently we *do* do that here nowadays.

"In some ways it seems like this city is the best it's ever been and the worst it's ever been," a friend of mine was saying the other day. "Not to get too *Tale of Two Cities* about it."

254

I knew what he meant. We have never had a more vibrant arts community here, a more diverse population, a livelier food and entertainment scene, or a higher per capita density of writers (song- and regular)—a density of writers that surely rivals Brooklyn's. At the same time, our downtown is a garish, bedazzled strip of neon and rooftop bars, and our working-class and poor neighbors have fewer and fewer places to live as condos and McMansions spring up everywhere and out-of-town investors drive up the cost of modest houses, hoping to cash out in the short-term-rental market. Don't even get me started on the traffic.

Neither the best of Nashville nor the worst of Nashville is what *Nashville* gives us, but watching the show, we feel ourselves poised in the same kind of interstitial space: the gap between reality and imagination, between what we are and what we might yet become. For *Nashville,* as Loretta Lynn once sang, we've reached the beginning of the end; for the real Nashville, there are many choices still to make as the city grows and grows and grows.

I left the *Nashville* warehouse sale with a coffee mug the cashier didn't even charge me for. ("Let's say twenty-five cents," she said. "Oh, make it ten," another cashier threw out. "You know what? Just take it," the cashier finally said.) The plain white mug isn't emblazoned with the show's logo or the stars' likenesses, but it's the size I especially like, and the handle fits my hand. And maybe an unadorned coffee cup is the perfect emblem for a show like *Nashville* anyway—a kind of miniature scrim for projection, a canvas for memory, or imagination, or whatever it is we think we want to be.

"BEAUTY HERSELF
IS BLACK"

The ballet Attitude: Lucy Negro Redux *is a forceful
claiming of female desire and sexual self-determination.*

FEBRUARY 18, 2019

T his is an arts town, and artistic miracles happen here
with some regularity, but last weekend's miracle was
not the usual kind. Watching John Prine, at the age
of seventy-two, dance onstage after a three-hour performance
at the legendary Ryman Auditorium—that's a quintessentially
Nashville kind of miracle. Watching *Lucy Negro, Redux*, a
poetry collection by an African American woman, come to life
as *Attitude: Lucy Negro Redux*, a ballet scored by an African
American woman and danced by an African American woman?
That's the kind of miracle Nashville has never seen before.

The project started with Caroline Randall Williams,
who became fascinated as a graduate student with a theory
advanced by Duncan Salkeld, a Shakespeare scholar at
the University of Chichester, that the mysterious Dark
Lady of Shakespeare's sonnets wasn't a white woman with
a dark complexion at all—she was a Black woman called
"Black Luce," or "Lucy Negro," who owned a brothel in
Shakespearean London. When Shakespeare wrote in Sonnet
132, "Then will I swear beauty herself is black," he meant,
actually, Black.

There are different theories about the identity of the
sonnets' Dark Lady—just as there is much speculation about

the identity of the "fair youth" to whom so many of the earlier sonnets are addressed—but this one ignited the young poet's imagination. Ms. Williams descends from Nashville literary royalty: her mother is the novelist and songwriter Alice Randall; her paternal grandfather was the civil rights activist Avon Williams; a great-grandfather was the Harlem Renaissance poet (and later Fisk University writer-in-residence) Arna Bontemps. But Caroline Randall Williams also descends from white men who raped her Black ancestors. She carries in her very DNA the conflict at the heart of *Lucy Negro, Redux*: What does it mean for a woman to be both desired and reviled for the color of her skin?

A university research grant allowed Ms. Williams to join Dr. Salkeld's search through primary documents for definitive proof that Lucy Negro was indeed Shakespeare's Dark Lady. Proof was not forthcoming, but poetry was.

The poems in *Lucy Negro, Redux*—first published in 2015 and reissued last week in an expanded edition by Third Man Books—defy genre. Or, rather, they wander with intense prepossession through many genres. Part lyrical narrative, part bluesy riff, part schoolyard chant, and part holy incantation, the book is an unflinching investigation of otherness and a dead-sexy exploration of the intersection of identity and desire. Above all it is a witty and audacious rejoinder to literary history and its systematic suppression of female voices. Especially Black female voices.

It's a powerful collection, but it is not the kind of book that you might naturally think of as source material for an original ballet. Unless, that is, you're Paul Vasterling, the visionary artistic director of the Nashville Ballet, where a transcendent dancer named Kayla Rowser—a fierce intensity of muscle and bone and spirit, untroubled by gravity—was perfectly positioned to play Lucy as Caroline Randall Williams had imagined her.

Before long, Mr. Vasterling had persuaded Rhiannon Giddens—a conservatory-trained MacArthur Fellow, though she may be better known as a cofounder of the Carolina Chocolate Drops and as a recurring character on the television drama *Nashville*—to write the score. Working in collaboration with the jazz composer Francesco Turrisi, Ms. Giddens also performed the music onstage while Ms. Williams herself entered the performance space as narrator and muse and, at times, the still center to a swirling human kaleidoscope of dancing bodies.

I am still pondering the artistic miracle that unfolded before me last weekend, as part of a sold-out series, before the most diverse audience I have ever seen at the Tennessee Performing Arts Center's Polk Theater. *Attitude: Lucy Negro Redux* was a beautifully choreographed ballet, but it was more than a ballet: it was also a spoken-word incantation and a showcase for the musical genius of Rhiannon Giddens. It was a love story, but it was more than a love story: it was also a forceful and pointed claiming of female desire—for authority, for sovereignty, for sexual self-determination.

The Nashville literary world is small enough that most writers know, or at least have met, the other writers who live here. I first met Caroline Randall Williams when she was four years old, the year I met her mother. As part of my job as editor of a literary publication here, I celebrated the arrival of *Lucy Negro, Redux* when it was published the first time, in a tiny print run from a tiny press.

But I was not at all prepared for *Lucy Negro Redux*, the ballet. There is nothing tiny about it, or about the scope of its artistic ambitions. It is a full-throated, full-bodied exploration of love and desire, exultation and loss, belonging and expulsion, ownership and autonomy. A mixed-media, multigenre embodiment of a scholarly theory about an arcane point of literary history might not seem like fertile ground for enchantment, but it was absolutely transformative.

Who is Lucy Negro? We may never know whether she was Shakespeare's Dark Lady, but we know that she is Kayla Rowser, who has spent her entire professional life in a field that rarely elevates a dancer with brown skin. We know that she is Rhiannon Giddens, who moves fluidly between African diaspora music and American symphony halls. We know that she is Caroline Randall Williams, an African American woman with depraved white ancestors, an African American woman who grew up in a literary household and learned to love Shakespeare when she was still a child.

And now Lucy Negro is Nashville, too, for she has taught us something about who we are. Flawed and impossible as this city may be on so many scores, it is also a place where a choreographer and a poet and a composer can come together with an entire ballet company to make something wildly original, something so unlike anything else that all description falls short of its otherworldly reality. A place where, when the curtain drops, the whole city cries out: "Brava! Brava! Oh, brava!"

THE DAY THE MUSIC DIED

*Unchecked growth has claimed Bobby's Idle Hour, the
last live-music venue on Nashville's fabled Music Row.*

January 21, 2019

I am not a musician, or even an aspiring musician, but I moved to Nashville because of music. One of my college roommates was in graduate school at Vanderbilt and invited me to visit, and my fiancé tagged along. He was, and still is, a picker himself, and he expected to fall in love with Music City; he even packed his résumé.

Katy Ginanni, my college friend, lived on 17th Avenue South, in the section called Music Square West. It's part of a rectangle of streets that collectively form Nashville's fabled Music Row, which became the heart of Nashville's music industry—not just country music, but also gospel music and Christian music and, in recent decades, pretty much every other kind of music. Music Row is the very definition of a cultural center, but Nashville's cultural center didn't spring from the mind of an urban planner. It grew up organically, as music-related businesses opened in the mid-twentieth century to capitalize on the growing popularity of country music.

Centered on 16th and 17th Avenues, Music Row was originally the site of recording studios (many of which have lately closed or moved elsewhere), music-publishing firms, talent and publicity agencies, and booking offices, all nestled among old bungalows and churches and human-scale commercial buildings. B. B. King and Loretta Lynn and Dolly Parton and

Elvis Presley and Charley Pride all recorded there, which you probably know, but so did Bob Dylan and Neil Young and Simon & Garfunkel and the Beach Boys, which you might not. In 2015, the National Trust for Historic Preservation designated the whole district "a national treasure."

Tour buses drive up and down the streets of Music Row, their guides telling tourists the stories they came to town to hear. But the city's explosive growth in the last decade has imperiled its own beating heart, with quaint Music Row houses and historic Music Row studios falling again and again to developers who put up fancy condominiums and trendy restaurants and shiny office buildings in their place, despite concerted efforts by individuals and historic preservation nonprofits to save the Row's character. In 2014, we nearly lost the iconic RCA Studio A.

My friend Katy's apartment was within walking distance of the Country Music Hall of Fame (it has since moved downtown), as well as seemingly innumerable storefront "museums" dedicated to specific stars. Broke as we were, we paid to have our picture made with a wax museum figure of Dolly Parton, just to have a souvenir of our visit. It was so hot in the building that even Dolly's wax doppelgänger is sweating in that Polaroid photo.

We loved the kitsch, but what really sold us was the music. We had arrived in Nashville in time for a music festival called Summer Lights, an act-after-act marvel of unfathomable talent. Music and cigarette smoke poured out of the neighborhood bars, and during our visit we stopped in to tap our feet and drink a beer at I don't know how many of them. We especially loved a shabby little tavern called Bobby's Idle Hour.

Back in those days Bobby's occupied a trailer, which I remember thinking was like a living stereotype, the kind of place that becomes the center of the story every time you talk about the time you went to Nashville. It's nothing like the music-themed bars that now line the tourist center known as Lower Broad, where neon and big-hat country hold sway— the part of Nashville that the journalist Steve Cavendish, writing in *Rolling Stone*, calls the "bar industrial complex."

Bobby's is an altogether different kind of bar. It began life simply as the Idle Hour. By 1978, when Bobby Herald bought it and added his name to the sign, it had already been on the Row for decades, a place where songwriters and neighbors and music scouts and industry regulars gathered. On weekend afternoons, people would bring their kids to hear the music.

In 2005, the Idle Hour was evicted from its longtime site—a condominium complex sits there now—and Bobby Herald and his wife, Dianne, moved the bar to its current location on 16th Avenue, eight doors down from the old trailer. Bobby died later that year, but Dianne kept the bar going. It still has autographed headshots of musicians taped to the walls, interspersed with dollar bills signed by guests. Hundreds, maybe thousands, of dollar bills, many yellowed by smoke from the years before the bar banned smoking.

Lizard Thom Case, seventy-two years old, bought the place in 2013 after Dianne retired, but he'd been a regular there for years before he bought it—so much of a regular that Dianne handpicked him to be Bobby's "steward," as Mr. Case calls himself. Even he doesn't remember how the tradition of taping dollar bills to the walls began: "I don't know how it started, but it grew like a fungus," he said. His best guess: "Tourists love this place so much, they just want to leave some part of themselves here." Visitors still come back years later, he said, and take selfies next to their own signed bills.

Last summer Mr. Case's landlord announced that he was selling the site and four adjacent buildings to a developer. (All five evicted businesses are quintessentially Music City: a clothing store called So Nashville, a guitar repair shop, a music academy, a music publisher, and Bobby's.) Short of the kind of eleventh-hour miracle that saved Studio A, Bobby's Idle Hour ("The only live music venue on Music Row!" according to its website) would end its seven-decade run, and yet another office building would rise in its place.

"Nashville doesn't have preservation tools that other cities use as a matter of course," Carolyn Brackett, senior field officer for the National Trust for Historic Preservation, told *The Tennessean* last summer. "There are practical solutions that would balance development with the preservation of Music Row's historic fabric and retain the music businesses that fill them. We urge Mayor Briley and Metro Nashville leaders to adopt them before it's too late."

For the current iteration of Bobby's Idle Hour, it's already too late. Last fall Bobby's was named to the "Nashville 9," an annual list of the most endangered historic places in Nashville, but this time no miracle was forthcoming. Mr. Case has until the end of the month to clear everything out.

It was never his plan to retire: "If we'd been able to stay in this venue, this particular building, I could've kept this bar another ten years," he said. "I love it. I love nurturing the songwriters. I love setting up these great nights of music. It's been my life."

I stopped by the bar on January 12, the last day it was open to the public, and spoke with Josh Distad, twenty-nine, a songwriter and Minnesota native who's been tending bar at Bobby's for the past four years. He and three other investors, all Bobby's regulars, had just bought the contents of the bar, along with its name, from Lizard Case. They hope to open again at a new location in the summer. Mr. Distad isn't worried about making Bobby's a success; Bobby's is already a success, and he's been studying what makes it work. But he recognizes the forces that he and his partners are up against, too.

They're considering a site just around the corner from the current Idle Hour, but there may be zoning issues to address there—it's near a church—and other obstacles to repurposing the building as a tavern.

The chief obstacle is Nashville itself. The five-year lease the building's owner has offered is within the new owners' price range, but they know they may well be priced out of the neighborhood again as soon as the lease is up, and they can't afford to buy. "The real estate in this area—real estate in the city, really—is so high now that a small mom-and-pop shop just can't succeed," Mr. Distad said. "The lowest property we found on the market in this area is listed for a million dollars." Even so, he believes the right place will turn up in time.

The death of a neighborhood bar in a growing city is in no way a tragedy. There are much more disruptive consequences to poorly planned growth: the loss of affordable workforce housing, the destruction of a vibrant tree canopy that offsets the effects of greenhouse gases, destabilized communities, and debilitating strains on aging infrastructure, among others. But cultural continuity does matter. Bobby's Idle Hour is "part of the fabric of this town," said Carolyn Lethgo, twenty-nine, a Middle Tennessee native and one of Mr. Distad's coinvestors. "We just want to carry on the meaning and the legacy of this place."

It's a quite a legacy. Before you even walk in the door, the big plywood guitar out front tells you that Bobby's Idle Hour is the place you've been looking for, the kind of place that makes you pack up and move to a new city to start your life all over again. In part because of Bobby's, my husband and I have been here thirty-one years, our entire adult lives.

Jonathan Long, seventy-two, is a songwriter from upstate New York who came here in 1971. He's also one of the Idle Hour's longtime bartenders. "I've been working here twenty years," he told me, "but I've been drinking here forty-seven." He plans to be at work at the new Idle Hour, too, wherever it lands, even if that's not on Music Row.

I asked Mr. Long if the Nashville moment had passed, if it's too late now for a songwriter with a dream to make a life here. He wasn't entirely hopeless: "If it's something you want to do, don't even bother to come here," he said. "If it's something you have to do, you might want to come. But if it's something you *are*, get your ass down here. It has to be who you are, or it's not going to work."

AFTER WAR, THREE CHORDS AND THE TRUTH

Songwriter Mary Gauthier's new album, cowritten with American veterans, suggests an unconventional way through trauma.

MARCH 5, 2018

T he first time I heard Mary Gauthier sing, it was 2005 and a song called "Mercy Now" was playing on the car radio. My father had been dead two years by then, but my eyes filled instantly with tears at the first line—"My father could use a little mercy now"—and I had to pull over to the side of the road because I couldn't see to drive. "I love my father; he could use some mercy now," sang Mary Gauthier as I sat behind the wheel of my still-running car and wept.

The first time I heard Mary Gauthier talk, it was 2016 and she was asking a question at the Southern Festival of Books. The fiction writer Odie Lindsey was reading from *We Come to Our Senses*, a story collection about American veterans after the first Gulf War. When he stopped to take comments from the audience, a woman in the front row asked one of the most insightful questions I'd ever heard at an author event. Later, walking down the wide marble stairs of the Nashville Public Library, I caught up with her and introduced myself. "I'm Mary Gauthier," she responded, holding out her hand.

"Oh, my God," I said. "I love you!"

"I love you, too," she said.

Apparently, when a complete stranger says "I love you" to Mary Gauthier, she says "I love you" right back.

This impulse to empathy courses through her new album, *Rifles & Rosary Beads*. Cowritten with American veterans or military family members, these songs are the result of an innovative nonprofit called SongwritingWith:Soldiers, which pairs master songwriters people like Beth Nielsen Chapman, Jay Clementi, Marshall Crenshaw, and Gary Nicholson—with servicemen and -women who have returned from war physically, emotionally, or spiritually wounded.

"There's no diagnoses or assessments," said Ms. Gauthier, a Louisiana native whose name is pronounced "go-SHAY." Instead, it's the opportunity to turn trauma into art. By the end of every weekend-long retreat, each veteran's experience has been transformed into a song.

In some ways Ms. Gauthier is ideally suited for this work. An alcoholic and addict in recovery for twenty-seven years, she understands confusion and shame, powerlessness and anger. "I've always been drawn to the hard story, the trauma, because I think art can turn it around," she said in an interview. "In a lot of ways, songwriting helped save my life. Recovery stabilized me; songwriting gave me a purpose."

In other ways, cowriting with military veterans might not seem like a natural fit for Ms. Gauthier, a lesbian and an outspoken liberal who received death threats because of the anti-war sentiment in "Mercy Now." When the song was first released, Ms. Gauthier had to call the FBI because trolls were sending her pictures of beheadings with captions that read, "Tick-tock, tick-tock."

When SongwritingWith:Soldiers founder Darden Smith first invited her to be part of a veterans' retreat, she hesitated: "I had a head full of stereotypes of what I thought a soldier was." What she learned is that the military is a microcosm of American culture: "It's a lot of women, people of color, gay men and lesbians, Hispanic, all faiths," she said. "It isn't the straight, white-guy conservative who likes to shoot shit up." On songwriting weekends, politics is nowhere to be found.

Each veteran or family member is paired with a songwriter, a process that begins with the participants' own stories. Some of the veterans take longer than others to arrive at a place of candor, but eventually the songwriter's basic questions ("When and where did you serve?" "What branch were you in?" "What did you see when you got there?") give way to harder questions ("Is there something you feel deep inside you need to say?"), and the shape of a song begins to emerge.

Once Ms. Gauthier picks up the guitar and begins fiddling with a melody, that's when the floodgates open: "Melody's like tweezers that go into the infection and pull out the wounded part," she said. "You can almost not stay silent in the face of a melody that matches your emotion. You feel seen. There's a myth that soldiers don't talk. Well, this generation will."

My father-in-law, who served in Korea, often points out that the generation after his was the first not to face the draft, and I wonder if this is the difference Ms. Gauthier means, but she shakes her head. "There's before Oprah and after Oprah," she said. The willingness to voice vulnerability is just part of the American psyche now.

The songs in *Rifles & Rosary Beads*—chosen from among the roughly forty Gauthier has cowritten with veterans during the last five years—reflect the full gamut of the military experience: fighting, injury, death, comradery, sexual assault, survivor's guilt, fear, and moral trauma, which happens when servicemembers can't reconcile what they've done with the people they believe themselves to be. Many of the songs wrestle with the unexpected challenges of homecoming.

"Soldiering On," cowritten with Marines veteran Jennifer Marino, points out how the attitude that can save your life in wartime ("Suck it up, shut it down / It don't matter how you feel") is the same attitude that will eat you alive when the war is over: "But what saves you in the battle / Can kill you at home / A soldier, soldiering on."

A song cowritten with Beth Nielsen Chapman and the wives of six service members, "The War After the War" acknowledges the sacrifice of military spouses: "Who's gonna care for the ones who care for the ones who went to war?" the song asks in its first line.

In a documentary directed by Joshua Britt and Neilson Hubbard about the making of *Rifles & Rosary Beads*, Josh Geartz says he was suicidal after he returned from Iraq but that his experience with Ms. Gauthier gave him hope. "The session that I had, where I was able to tell Mary, who I wrote with, things that no one on this planet knows—that's kind of where that flicker of hope started. Right there, that moment."

Gauthier does not use the term *healing* in connection with these retreats: "*Heal* is so woo-woo," she said, and probably unrealistic in the context of war. Songs, even powerful songs cowritten with veterans, will not eliminate the tragedy of veteran suicide, and Gauthier knows that. "The hope is that this is a rung" on the ladder out of a dark hole, she said. Just the first rung. "But a rung is a big damn deal if you haven't been able to find one."

Most of the servicemembers who cowrote the songs on *Rifles & Rosary Beads* are not musicians, but Mr. Geartz, who cowrote "Still on the Ride," is a skilled harmonica player. At an album-release performance at the Franklin Theatre on February 23, Mr. Geartz rolled onto the stage in his wheel-chair and performed with Ms. Gauthier on his own song, as well as on Woody Guthrie's "This Land Is Your Land," the final song of the set.

When I left the theater that night, several dozen people were already lined up at the autograph signing table. I had a feeling a lot of them were just waiting to tell Mary Gauthier how much they love her.

PROUD GRADUATE
OF STATE U.

*Sometimes the best school isn't the "elite" college at the
top of the national rankings. It's the public
university just down the road.*

MARCH 25, 2019

News of the recent college-bribery scandal broke the
same week the University of Tennessee announced
it would be offering free tuition to Tennessee families earning less than $50,000 a year. The announcement
came the day my two younger sons were finishing up their
UT midterms and packing to come back to Nashville for
spring break, where home-cooked meals and a fair amount of
yardwork awaited them.

My husband is a schoolteacher, and I work for a humanities nonprofit. This work will never make us rich, but we're
doing just fine, and the new tuition program at our sons' university won't affect us. But sending two children to college at
once is still a stretch. Sometimes I think of the financial planner we hired when I was pregnant with our youngest child. We
hadn't started a college-savings plan yet and needed help sort-
ing out the bewildering array of options. The financial planner
looked at our paperwork, saw what we were earning, and said
flatly, "You can't afford to send three kids to college."

Somehow we have. Our oldest, a history major, had his
heart set on a liberal arts college. We managed to make it work
only because he lived at home for the first few years, and only

because my mother died and left just enough money behind to put tuition within reach, if barely. But our son also worked at least twenty hours a week during the school year, and full-time every summer, and he paid for much of his education himself.

That liberal arts college ended up being a great choice for him, but my husband and I worried about what we'd do if his younger brothers, only two years apart in school, also wanted expensive private colleges. Fortunately, our middle son's top choice was the University of Tennessee, which has a strong engineering program. Later, our youngest made the same choice, partly because he wanted to be in school with his brother again, and partly because he wanted a big university with a wide array of majors to explore.

The idea of a college search would have been foreign to me as a high school senior. Of the two flagship state universities, I picked my mother's alma mater and was admitted simply by having my ACT scores sent there. When I got to Auburn University in the fall of 1980, Pell Grants, work-study assignments, and low-interest federal loans were still plentiful enough that students like me—people not impoverished enough or brilliant enough to earn a full ride—could nevertheless get a good education, even if their parents couldn't afford to pay a dime. It never crossed my mind that I was "settling" for something less than an elite education. I was grateful beyond belief to be going to college at all.

How I wish I had the words, even now, to explain what a gift those years were. I took an overload almost every quarter because adding courses didn't cost more, and it was impossible to choose from among all the offerings. I wanted to learn everything, read everything, think about everything. And everything seemed to be right there for the taking on that rural campus in the piedmont of Alabama.

Some of my professors were boring, sure, and some were ancient cranks who hadn't done a minute's scholarship in decades. But most others opened their office doors, leaned back in their chairs, and carried on the conversation long after class, as long as I still had questions. One professor conducted a one-student correspondence course by mail, just for fun, the summer before I was a sophomore. Another offered a bunch of us the guest quarters at her house in the country as a quiet place to study for exams. Still another convened a Latin literature class at 7:00 a.m., five days a week, because there were only four students in the whole university who wanted to read literature in Latin, and the university wouldn't schedule a class for only four students. We all signed up for Latin as an independent-study course, and we met in that professor's office, where he taught us, unpaid, for nearly two years.

At Auburn, I learned to run a literary publication—the kind of work I still do today—and I made lifelong friends. I got a good education there—good enough, at least, to get me into graduate school at the kind of elite university that's at the heart of today's cheating scandal. But that elite university was also a school where I did not belong. It was just too far from home, too far from the soil my bare feet longed for. When I transferred to the University of South Carolina for my master's degree, I found the same thing I'd found at Auburn: everything I needed was right there—if I looked for it—and it felt like home.

Yes, state universities have their problems, and those problems can be profound. Cash-strapped legislatures too often balance their budgets by cutting funds to higher education, resulting in catastrophic tuition hikes. Provincial yahoos too often serve as university trustees or administrators, energetically erecting barriers to the kind of wide-ranging curiosity that a university education is supposed to foster. Tenured professors retire and are too often replaced by adjuncts so underpaid and so shamefully overburdened that their work amounts to exploitation. And that's just for starters.

Nevertheless, against all odds, the real heart of a college education—the bond born of shared intellectual exploration between teachers and curious students, between curious students and each other—remains intact, if only in pockets of campus life, at every state university I know. My brother and sister-in-law are professors at a state university, and I have friends who work at other state universities and community colleges across the region. To a person, their commitment to their students and to their own research and creative work is an inspiration. I would entrust my children's education to them without a moment's hesitation.

In fact, I already have. My sons are getting much the same kind of education at the University of Tennessee that I got so many years ago at Auburn and that my husband got at the University of Georgia. With some exceptions—just as there were decades ago—our sons are being challenged intellectually and supported emotionally. They are making friends who will be their friends for life.

As with my oldest son, a large state university isn't the right fit for every student. There are many kinds of schools and many kinds of students, and I understand that. What I don't understand is why so many people seem to think you can't get a good education at a rank-and-file state university— not Berkeley or the University of Virginia, but still the kind of school the vast majority of young people in this country would feel grateful and honored to attend.

In the end, students who want an education will get an education wherever they go to school. No cheating required.

AND PLAY LIKE A
GIRL SHE DID

*Vanderbilt's Sarah Fuller is the first woman to play
Power 5 football. She's been a long time coming.*

DECEMBER 5, 2020

When Sarah Fuller stepped onto the field at the University of Missouri on November 28, she wasn't wearing the jersey she normally wears as a goalkeeper for Vanderbilt University's women's soccer team. On that Saturday after Thanksgiving, she was wearing full pads and a Commodores football jersey. Her helmet was emblazoned with the words "Play Like a Girl."

Ms. Fuller kicked off for the Commodores at the beginning of the game's second half. As she did, she also kicked through a glass ceiling, becoming the first woman to play in a Power 5 football game. (Other women have played college football, though none at the elite level of the Power 5 conferences.)

This wasn't the culmination of a young woman's life-long goal, and it wasn't a publicity stunt by a team in the midst of a humiliating season. Coronavirus quarantines had left Vanderbilt without a kicker, and Ms. Fuller, a twenty-one-year-old senior from Wylie, Texas, was the team's best hope. The Commodores hadn't won a single football game all season, while Vanderbilt women's soccer had just won the Southeastern Conference Division 1 championship, its first title since 1994. And Ms. Fuller was a powerful kicker for the championship team.

Though she'd been practicing with the football team for less than a week, she knew exactly what she was doing: "Let's make history," she tweeted before the game.

Derek Mason, the Commodores' head coach, said in a postgame news conference that he didn't tap Ms. Fuller for a date with history: "Listen, I'm not about making statements," he said. "This was out of necessity."

Necessity. That team needed Sarah Fuller much the way the United States of America needed Rosie the Riveter during World War II.

For days after the game, I found myself thinking again and again of Ms. Fuller, of the confidence in her smile as she held a football helmet emblazoned with a message that was personal. ("Play Like a Girl" is a reference to a nonprofit that promotes sports and STEM opportunities for girls.) I thought of the faith the Commodores had put in her—not because a woman had never played college football at that level before, but because Vanderbilt desperately needed a kicker, and Sarah Fuller can kick the holy hell out of a ball.

I thought about the time I tried out for my high school's football team, about how when I reported for practice, the coach kept shaking his head and saying: "Are you serious? Are you serious?" over and over again until he finally told me where I could pick up my pads.

As it happens, I wasn't serious, at least not about joining the football team. It was February 1978, not quite six years after Title IX of the Education Amendments of 1972 was signed into law. The legislation forbade institutions receiving federal funds—virtually all public schools and universities— from discriminating on the basis of gender. I was an aspiring writer, not an aspiring athlete, and I wanted to make everyone *believe* I was serious about football so I could write a story about it for the school paper. Title IX meant I could play football if I wanted to. Was Alabama ready for a girl football player?

All I can say is thank God Twitter didn't exist forty-two years ago because Alabama was definitely not ready for a girl football player.

I told Ms. Fuller that story on a Zoom call earlier this week and asked if she had experienced the same disbelief as a young woman growing up in the South. Her response was measured. "I would like to say the narrative's changed a little bit," she said. "I'd like to say that, and then again there's people on social media that are like, 'You're not supposed to be out there' and all this stuff. But there's so much more positive around it now. There's so many more people pressing and being like: 'No, this needs to be the norm. This needs to be what we should expect from now on.'"

Ms. Fuller is not bothered by the blowback on social media: "The negative is just a waste of my time," she said. "I have worked hard to get where I am, and I was in the right spot at the right time to be called up on the football team, and I've been working really hard to perform for them. So at the end of the day I don't care what the negative is."

Blowback, I am thankful to report, isn't all Ms. Fuller has gotten. The other Vanderbilt players welcomed her to the team, according to quarterback Mike Wright. "I can 100 percent ensure that Sarah was accepted with open arms," he told reporters after the game.

Support has also poured in from other athletes and from women in all manner of fields who know something about competing in a man's world: "Thank you, Sarah, for helping to prove that women and girls belong on every playing field—quite literally," Hillary Clinton tweeted. In addition to receiving congratulations from every corner of the country, Ms. Fuller was also named an SEC Special Teams Player of the Week and was nominated for the Capital One Orange Bowl-FWAA Courage Award.

If this were a made-for-TV movie, Sarah Fuller would have led the winless Commodores to an unlikely victory. In real life, Missouri shut out Vandy with a final score of 41-0. And in real life Ms. Fuller's second-half kickoff was her only kick of the game—the Commodores never got into field goal range. But there's one part of this imaginary TV script that Ms. Fuller seems to have played with a natural gift: the passionate halftime speech. "I was like, 'We need to be cheering each other on,'" she told ESPN's Courtney Cronin. "'We need to be lifting each other up. That's what a team's about.'"

As Mr. Wright noted, "I mean, you can take a leader out of their sport, but at the end of the day she's still a leader."

This is the glory of Title IX and all other federal civil rights legislation, especially in parts of the country—here in the American South, for example—where barriers are so often slow to fall. Such laws don't merely open opportunities for the people whose rights have traditionally been ignored or openly denied. They also help to create a society where hard work and natural gifts can benefit us all. A football team needed Sarah Fuller. Thanks to Title IX, Sarah Fuller had the training and the skills and the pure, heart-lifting confidence to step up.

WHAT IS A SOUTHERN
WRITER, ANYWAY?

*Hint: it has nothing to do with screen doors
or dirt yards or sweet tea.*

From time to time, a debate resurfaces in Southern literary circles about whether there can still be a recognizable literature of the South in an age of mass media and Walmart. The twenty-first-century South would be unrecognizable to the Agrarian poets, whose 1930 manifesto, *I'll Take My Stand*, set out many of the principles that still cling like ticks to the term "Southern writer." Far more urban, far more ethnically and culturally and politically diverse, the South today is no longer a place defined by sweet tea and slamming screen doors, and its literature is changing, too. "It is damn hard to put a pipe-smoking granny or a pet possum into a novel these days and get away with it," the novelist Lee Smith once said.

I don't spend a lot of time wondering about the defining characteristic of the Southern writer because there is surely no single quality that defines Southern writing. But reading *People Only Die of Love in Movies: Film Writing by Jim Ridley*, a new book from Vanderbilt University Press, has got me to thinking about the question.

Most readers of *The New York Times* have probably never heard of Jim Ridley, but he was a hero in this town. A local boy who grew up in nearby Murfreesboro, he started contributing book reviews to *The Tennessean*, Nashville's daily newspaper, while he was in middle school. (In his take on Mary Stewart's Arthurian trilogy, he notes that Stewart's Merlin "speaks like a combination of the worst elements of John Cheever, a used-car salesman and Abigail Van Buren." He had just turned fourteen when he wrote that review.)

Mr. Ridley studied journalism and literature at Middle Tennessee State University, his hometown college. After he graduated in 1989, he started writing for the *Nashville Scene*, our local alt-weekly newspaper. When he died in 2016, he was the paper's editor. He had never lived anywhere other than Middle Tennessee.

There wasn't a single aspect of cultural life in this town that Jim Ridley didn't chronicle with originality and wit and some of the most graceful sentences ever committed to print. During the nearly twenty years I knew him, I never ceased to marvel that my unrelentingly humble friend was the same linguistic powerhouse who kept goading this city into becoming more than the sleepy backwater of country music and Bible publishing it believed itself to be. The editor of *People Only Die of Love in Movies*, Steve Haruch, writes in its introduction, "Long before Nashville ever appeared on the national hip-city radar, Jim saw and highlighted the city's strengths while also holding the city and the people in it to the highest standards."

This is what the truly great writers—the great journalists, the great novelists, the great poets, the great playwrights—always do: they know their communities from the inside out, as full members, and they tell the truth about what they know.

Great writers everywhere do the same thing, but the South's legacy of slavery and its overt and enduring racism make the Southern writer's truth especially urgent—never more so than now, when our president and his enablers daily speak the unapologetic language of white supremacy.

People Only Die of Love in Movies isn't the only posthumous work of literary art coming out this month by a Tennessee writer who found his own hometown both vexing and endlessly fascinating: there's also *The Lost Country*, a new novel by William Gay, who lived almost his entire life in Hohenwald, just southwest of Nashville. "Mr. Gay wrote about rustic Tennessee with an inside observer's eye for local color and a hyperbolist's delight in regional idiosyncrasies," a 2012 obituary in *The Times* noted.

Among the living Tennessee homebodies with new releases, there's the Pulitzer Prize–winning biographer Jon Meacham, whose nonfiction book *The Soul of America: The Battle for Our Better Angels* was released in May. There's the novelist Kevin Wilson, who grew up and still lives on the Cumberland Plateau: his new story collection, *Baby, You're Gonna Be Mine*, will be published in August. There's the novelist Ann Patchett, whose new nonfiction book about Nashville, a joint project with the photographer Heidi Ross, is coming out in November. Ms. Patchett lives two blocks from where she grew up.

People can hardly help loving the hands that rocked their cradles or the landscapes that shaped their souls, but I doubt there's a single writer in the South for whom life here isn't a source of deep ambivalence. And yet all the writers I've mentioned have had opportunities to leave—and many actually did leave for a time before returning to stay.

It has all made me wonder: What if being a Southern writer has nothing to do with rural tropes or lyrical prose or a lush landscape or humid heat so thick it's hard to breathe?

What if being a Southern writer is foremost a matter of growing up in a deeply troubled place and yet finding it somehow impossible to leave? Of seeing clearly the failings of home and nevertheless refusing to flee?

I honestly don't know if I'm right about this. For one thing, Southerners don't hold the copyright on a close connection to home, and there are many exceptions to the rule. Historically, African American writers tended to leave the South as fast as they could, and for obvious reasons.

Still. Think about William Faulkner and Flannery O'Connor and Eudora Welty, the great pillars of what we think of as Southern literature. Among the living, think about the novelist Jesmyn Ward in Mississippi. Think about the novelists Josephine Humphreys and George Singleton in South Carolina. Think about Wendell Berry and Silas House and Bobbie Ann Mason and Frank X. Walker in Kentucky. Think about the playwright Katori Hall in Memphis, and the poets T. J. Jarrett and Caroline Randall Williams here in Nashville. They're all living and writing in the very places where they were born.

I think of my old friend Jim Ridley—I think of all these writers, old and young, living and dead—and here's what crosses my mind: Maybe being a Southern writer has always been more than stereotypes of ceiling fans and panting dogs in dirt yards. Maybe being a Southern writer is only a matter of loving a damaged and damaging place, of loving its flawed and beautiful people, so much that you have to stay there, observing and recording and believing, against all odds, that one day it will finally live up to the promise of its own good heart.

GRACELAND, AT LAST

For reasons I cannot explain, some part
of me needed to go there.

JANUARY 6, 2018

In 1986, Paul Simon released his seventh solo album, *Graceland*. One year later, my fiancé and I moved to Nashville. He was driving my father's secondhand panel van with the fake wood-grain wraparound made of shelf liner that masked the previous owner's business logo. Attached to the van was a trailer too heavy for the hitch. I was driving the Exploding Pinto, a nickname derived from that ancient model's fuel-tank fires, and on top of the Pinto were several hundred pounds of books, provisionally contained in a homemade roof rack built of two-by-fours.

Between South Carolina, where we had just finished graduate school, and Tennessee, where we would start our new teaching jobs, lay the Appalachian Mountains. Getting over them in one piece would be the first real test of our lives as fully employed adults.

Top-heavy and buffeted by winds, the chugging old Pinto struggled. My traveling companion—a cat who badly needed to pee but refused to use the litter box on the back seat—was perched on my headrest, her claws gripping my head as eighteen-wheelers barreled around us in the dark. In the cassette player on the passenger seat, Paul Simon was singing "Graceland." It is not too much to say that

"Graceland" got me safely over Monteagle Mountain when I was in danger of going over the edge.

I grew up in a house without a stereo, and my parents' car radio was always tuned to big band music, so my formative years were in no way informed by Elvis Presley. But you hear cheerful music just as you're thinking you might truly die, and you form a kind of bond with it. Driving over Monteagle Mountain with a cat latched to my head, I vowed to see Graceland someday. How lucky to be moving to the very state where Graceland could be found!

Decades passed, and we still hadn't made it. We once went to a conference in Memphis, but three hours after we checked in we got word of a death in the family, and so we got back in the car and headed home. Our babies—who were worse traveling companions than the cat—kept road trips confined to far-flung family reunions.

In 2010, when our oldest son chose a college in Memphis, I thought I would surely see Graceland at last. We packed up our two younger sons, then fourteen and twelve, and made a vacation of the college's Family Weekend. We toured the Stax Museum of American Soul Music, took a walk along the Mississippi River, visited the ducks in the fountain at the Peabody Hotel, ate ribs at the Rendezvous, and peeked into blues joints on Beale Street.

What we did not do was visit Graceland. Halfway through our tour, the kids rebelled. They did not want to pay homage to Dr. King at the National Civil Rights Museum. They did not want to visit Sun Records. Most of all, they did not want to visit Graceland. "It'll be fun," I said. "There's a Jungle Room." They said they'd rather go back to their brother's dorm and shoot each other with the Nerf guns they'd packed in lieu of clean underwear.

By the time we'd dropped them at the college, there wasn't time to make it to Graceland before closing, so my husband and I sat outside in the hotel hot tub and drank a bottle of wine out of plastic cups and looked at the gray Memphis skyline. How sharper than a serpent's tooth it is to have a thankless child who won't even go to Graceland with you.

Fast-forward another seven years. Our oldest son—who had transferred to another school after only a semester—was all grown up, the middle boy was in college, and the youngest was almost on his way. We were hosting an Australian exchange student, a teenage boy who loved American music. One day my husband said, "I wonder if the guys would like to go to Memphis." Unbelievably, they were game, and this time I didn't make the same mistake. First stop: Graceland.

It was not at all what I'd envisioned. Outside on a rainy Sunday in January, the crowd-control stanchions were entirely unnecessary, the massive parking lot nearly empty. In thirty years of waiting, had I inflated Graceland in my own mind? Had I read too much spiritual significance into its name, expecting some sort of blessing?

Then, like Alice through the looking glass, I stepped through a door still bearing a desiccated Christmas wreath, and that's when everything got awesome. Graceland's formal rooms are all white carpet and gold trimmings and mirrors— walls and walls of mirrors. With its hide-covered furniture and lamps hanging from chains and vines draping a stone wall, the Jungle Room did not disappoint, but downstairs was the real action: a room with three televisions embedded in the walls, a sectional sofa with sequin-bedecked pillows, and a mirror-topped coffee table bearing a bizarre porcelain creature of indeterminate origin gazing toward the door; a billiard room with walls and ceiling entirely upholstered in pleated floral fabric that might have been fashioned by a seamstress on mushrooms.

By today's measure of lavish wealth, Elvis's mansion would be dwarfed by any family home in an upscale suburb, but to a girl of the '70s who grew up poor enough for contact paper to seem like a reasonable way to embellish a used van, it was perfect. Walking past all those mirrors, I kept catching glimpses of myself, grinning.

Somehow it felt like more than checking off an item on a bucket list. Maybe it had something to do with a dawning sense that I was moving past the delayed gratifications of motherhood, past the time of putting off what I wanted to do. Or maybe it had something to do with coming full circle, of making a vow just as our marriage was beginning and finally seeing it through just as we were on the verge of being alone again. Mirror after mirror, there I was, right in the heart of Graceland: smiling and smiling and smiling.

ACKNOWLEDGMENTS

In 1983, when I was in college, I went home for Christmas a week late. Normally I'd leave campus immediately after my last exam, as soon as I could find a ride, but that year I was a senior, and extracurricular responsibilities trumped my desire to get home. As editor of the student magazine, I couldn't leave until the winter issue was finished and I'd safely delivered it to the printer.

The campus was so empty I half expected my footsteps to echo as I walked the sidewalks between the magazine's office in the student union and the university printshop. It was a drizzly day, chilly but not cold—characteristic weather for Alabama in early December—but I could not get over the uncharacteristic silence of a campus missing eighteen thousand students. Unnerved, I walked a little faster through the gloom.

When I reached the printshop, it was also eerily still. I handed my packet of pages over to the lone employee still working during the holidays: the silver-haired man who maintained the machinery. On sunny days he liked to take his break on a bench out front. He would lean back, his hands on his knees, perfectly still—no book; no companion; certainly, in those days, no phone. I asked him once what he was doing. "Oh," he said, "I'm just watching the pretty girls go by and thinking about the crucifixion of Jesus."

I hadn't been home long when I learned that the university president, acting on a tip from a printshop employee, had ordered the shop to impound our pages for violating the morality standards for campus publications. I had no idea what he was talking about. The issue contained the usual fare: essays about campus life, poems about love, atmospheric photographs. Nothing that could be considered troubling, much less immoral.

Then it came to me. Our essay selection included a piece about what it felt like to be gay at a conservative Southern university, where organizations like Campus Crusade for Christ held all the political power. Nurtured in the English department, where this kind of personal essay was routinely taught in freshman composition classes, I truly had not even considered that the piece might raise any hackles.

I had a pretty good idea of whose hackles it had raised.

There were other issues, too, it turned out, chiefly surrounding the use of a certain expletive in a short story—the sort of word, again, that came up with some regularity in the texts assigned in my own coursework. The fact that a university could forbid publication of student work containing the same language and the same subjects that were required reading at the very same university struck me as a cold irony. Not that an appreciation for irony was on visible display at the university printshop, or in the university president's office, either.

The ensuing fracas unfolded for months. Students signed petitions on behalf of the magazine. Other students signed petitions of support for the president. The communications board held hearings. Newspapers across the state covered the controversy. The ACLU threatened to sue the university for First Amendment violations. The resolution, when it finally came, was a classic example of winning the battle but losing the war: the president allowed the issue to be published, but the magazine lost its funding for the following year.

By then I'd decided what to do after graduation. I would be leaving the hidebound South as fast as I could shake its red dust from my sandals, and I would not be coming back.

ACKNOWLEDGMENTS

Readers of my previous book, *Late Migrations*, already know how poorly that plan went. I repatriated barely four months after stomping away, and I never left the South again. I didn't know it then, but I was home for good.

Thus did I learn my first lesson in the true nature of love.

⸺

I hope this book is a testament to that love, for I will never cease being grateful for what my homeland has given me: not just the beloved family and friends and places of my youth, but also the way my entire life has unfolded against this backdrop of home. If I had not come back to the South, everything I now hold onto most fervently—my marriage, my children, my friends, this work itself—would never have come within reach.

It is beyond my capacity to express how grateful I am to everyone at *The Times* for the trust that made this book possible. That gratitude extends up and down and across the masthead, from Kathleen Kingsbury and everyone on the opinion desk to Caroline Que and everyone in book development. But it lands most often, week after week after week, on my incomparable editor, Peter Catapano. Peter's ears are tuned to the music of language. His eyes never miss a typo. His understanding of narrative structure is innate and unerring. He is an ethical touchstone for a writer trying to address a complex and multifaceted culture, and every week he makes me a better writer.

I feel the same heartfelt gratitude to Joey McGarvey at Milkweed Editions, who found a way, through careful curation and sensitive ordering, to create a coherent whole from four years' worth of disparate columns, none of them written with a collection like this in mind. The slight variations between the versions of the essays found in this book and the versions that ran at *The Times* are the result of her unfailing ability to clarify a piece of writing—especially when significant time has passed between the news event that inspired the essay and now—and to remove authorial tics and repetitions that may be invisible in weekly installments but become annoying in collections. (Who knew I was so fond of the word "small"? Joey knew.)

In addition to the help of two different editors, this book has been blessed by the calm genius of my agent, Kristyn Keene Benton, who taught me how to write a book proposal and then shepherded it into reality; by the indefatigable organization of Cat Shook; by the unflagging support of Johanna Hynes and the team at Publishers Group West; and by the entire Milkweed staff, who make such beautiful books and work so hard to help them find their way to readers: Daniel Slager, Meagan Bachmayer, Shannon Blackmer, Tijqua Daiker, Meilina Dalit, Yanna Demkiewicz, Bailey Hutchinson, Claire Laine, Mary Austin Speaker, Anna Thorsen, Milan Wilson-Robinson, and Kachina Yeager.

I am especially thankful to all the Southerners who took the time to speak with me when I was writing these essays, and to all the journalists whose reporting underpins every opinion writer's work, not to mention a functioning democracy. I always link to articles I've relied on at *The Times* itself, but links aren't possible in a book, and I deeply regret their loss here. I give special thanks for Fiona Prine, who allowed me to quote several of John Prine's songs at length, and to Mary Gauthier, who did the same for her own.

The writers I love and whose work I admire are far too numerous to name, but I can't help singling out my writing-group partners for the inspiration of their own words: Ralph Bowden, Maria Browning, Susannah Felts,

Carrington Fox, Faye Jones, Susan McDonald, Mary Laura Philpott, and Chris Scott. Special thanks to Fernanda Moore, who read this whole collection in advance with the unique bilingual perspective of a native Southerner who has lived outside the South her entire adult life. As always, I owe my unending gratitude to Ann Patchett and Karen Hayes and all the compassionate, knowledgeable, and enthusiastic booksellers at Parnassus Books. The very best thing that could possibly happen to an author is to live in the town where Parnassus is her neighborhood bookstore.

And finally I come to my family, beside whom even this work I love so much pales in importance. I am grateful for our Nashville family: the Baileys, the Hills, the Michaels, the Tarkingtons, and the loving friends who have made this neighborhood a true home for twenty-six years. I have been grateful all my life for Billy Renkl and Lori Renkl, my earliest and still my closest friends, and my surest sources of inspiration. My children—Sam Moxley, Julie Hilton Moxley, Henry Moxley, and Joe Moxley—are the greatest gifts I have ever been given and my greatest reason for faith in the future. I give thanks to God for them every single day.

Most of all, I am grateful to Haywood Moxley, whose radiant goodness, unwavering strength, and steadfast love have been my shelter, my joy, and my ever-fixed mark since the moment we met. This book is for him.

MARGARET RENKL is the author of *Late Migrations*. Since 2017, she has been a contributing opinion writer for *The New York Times*, where her essays appear weekly. She was the founding editor of *Chapter 16*, the daily literary publication of Humanities Tennessee, and is a graduate of Auburn University and the University of South Carolina. She lives in Nashville.

milkweed
editions

Founded as a nonprofit organization in 1980, Milkweed
Editions is an independent publisher. Our mission is to
identify, nurture and publish transformative literature, and
build an engaged community around it.

Milkweed Editions is based in Bdé Óta Othúŋwe
(Minneapolis) within Mní Sota Makhóčhe, the traditional
homeland of the Dakhóta people. Residing here since
time immemorial, Dakhóta people still call Mní Sota
Makhóčhe home, with four federally recognized Dakhóta
nations and many more Dakhóta people residing in what
is now the state of Minnesota. Due to continued legacies
of colonization, genocide, and forced removal, generations
of Dakhóta people remain disenfranchised from their
traditional homeland. Presently, Mní Sota Makhóčhe has
become a refuge and home for many Indigenous nations
and peoples, including seven federally recognized Ojibwe
nations. We humbly encourage our readers to reflect upon
the historical legacies held in the lands they occupy.

milkweed.org

Interior design by Tijqua Daiker and Mary Austin Speaker
Typeset in Bulmer

Bulmer was created in the late 1780s or early 1790s.
This late "transitional" typeface was designed
by William Martin for William Bulmer,
who ran the Shakespeare Press.